TAX TIPS AND
TAX SHELTERS
FOR CANADIANS

Tax Tips and Tax Shelters for Canadians

Vlad Trkulja

INSOMNIAC PRESS

Library and Archives Canada Cataloguing in Publication

Trkulja, Vlad, 1969-
      Tax tips and tax shelters for Canadians / Vlad Trkulja.

Includes bibliographical references and index.
ISBN 978-1-897178-56-0

      1. Tax planning--Canada--Popular works. 2. Tax shelters--Canada--
Popular works. I. Title.

KE5682.T75 2008   343.7105'23   C2007-907657-2
KF6297.ZA2T75 2008

The publisher gratefully acknowledges the support of the Department of Canadian Heritage through the Book Publishing Industry Development Program.

Printed and bound in Canada

Insomniac Press, 192 Spadina Avenue, Suite 403
Toronto, Ontario, Canada, M5T 2C2
www.insomniacpress.com

Canadä

Acknowledgements

I would like to thank my parents, Svetozar and Draga, for choosing to immigrate to this great country in 1963 and providing me with the ability and support to obtain a wonderful education and create a joyous life for my family and me. They taught me a valuable lesson in life that hard work and ambition do pay off.

I would like to thank my wife, daughter, and son for providing me with the love and support for my many ventures and expeditions in life.

In addition, I would like to thank the many individuals who have become my clients over the last fifteen years whereby wealth has been created, taxes have been reduced, and friendships have been formed.

I wrote this book to provide Canadians with information to help them reduce their tax burden. It was produced with the help of Sanjiv Sawh, CFA, MBA, CFP, who is a managing partner at The Investment House of Canada. The chapters on Individual Pension Plans (IPPs) and Retirement Compensation Arrangements (RCAs) were written with the help of Marc Des Rosiers, FSA, FCIA of Aperion Consulting in Toronto. Marc's twenty-six years of actuarial experience has helped many Canadians structure IPPs and RCAs. His firm works with executives and business owners and provides them with complete solutions, including advice, legal documents, filings, administration, and actuarial certification. Marc can be reached at (416) 628-3743 or mdr@retireware.com.

Author's Contact Information
Vlad Trkulja
The Investment House of Canada Inc.
1033 Bay Street, Suite 221
Toronto, ON M5S 3A5
(416) 473-1090
vlad.trkulja@ihoc.ca
www.vladtrkulja.com

Disclaimer

The information contained in this book was gathered through many years of research. The intention of the material is to bring certain strategies, ideas, products, and services to the reader's attention. The reader should consult with a financial professional and a tax expert prior to implementing any information in the book, as the information is not intended to substitute competent comprehensive financial and professional advice. The information is provided as a general guide.

Table of Contents

Introduction

Since 1992, I have been in the financial services and investment brokerage industries providing Canadians with advice on how to manage their finances, structure investment portfolios, implement estate plans, and manage their overall family wealth.

I have come to realize over time that many people view Registered Retirement Savings Plans (RRSPs) as the only available tax shelter. In addition, many believe that few things are certain in life. They believe taxes and death cannot be avoided. They believe that an effective financial strategy simply means making their mortgage payments and contributing any excess funds to their RRSPs.

In addition to thinking that RRSPs are the only tax break or tax shelter available to Canadians, some people don't believe effective tax planning exists, while others believe it is only available to the wealthy. What these people don't realize is that many become wealthy by structuring effective tax planning in their working years when they have not yet accumulated the wealth so many desire.

Effective tax planning for Canadians is the basis of this book. It is written for you, whether you are looking to accumulate wealth, preserve your wealth, or increase your wealth. You will learn how to do so through the many tax planning strategies available in this country. Whether you are in a low tax bracket, middle tax bracket, or the highest of tax brackets, the information in this book can help reduce tax liability, generate tax refunds, and build and preserve wealth.

When properly implemented, the strategies discussed in this book are legitimate tax planning strategies recognized by many financial planners, financial experts, chartered accountants, actuaries, financial commentators, tax lawyers, and the Canada Revenue Agency.

Experienced financial planners must maintain the appropriate licences to be able to offer some of the products and services mentioned in this book. In addition to appropriate licences, the planners must be knowledgeable and work with financial institutions that have access to financial experts and some of the products and services mentioned. Ensure your planner has access to products, plans, and services, including flow-through investments, corporate class funds, ROC funds, prescribed annuities, Retirement Compensation Arrangements, Individual Pension Plans, immigration trusts, insurance tax shelters, and some or all of the things mentioned in the forthcoming chapters.

Chapter 1

Marginal Tax Rates and the Taxation of Investment Income

As your personal taxable income increases, the amount of tax paid as a percentage also increases. This means that income is taxed at different rates, and you pay less tax as a percentage of income that is in a low tax bracket and more tax as a percentage when income is in a higher tax bracket.

Canadian marginal tax rates increase as your taxable income increases. It is the total of both federal and provincial taxes, and it represents the rate of tax you pay on each additional dollar of income earned.

Marginal tax brackets should be understood by those who want to ensure successful and efficient financial and income planning and, more specifically, for those interested in tax-effective income-splitting strategies. See the marginal tax rate tables for 2007 in the appendix.

Calculating Your Tax Liability
To determine the amount of tax you must pay, you must add up all your sources of income including things such as salary, interest, dividends, and other sources of income and then subtract the various deductions such as RRSP contributions, deductible interest expenses, and other allowable expenses.

Income is not all taxed at the same rate. Canadian dividends and capital gains are taxed at more favourable rates than interest income and foreign income. In light of the different tax treatment, you should look beyond an investment's pre-tax rate of return and instead focus on the after-tax return. For example, a GIC or bond with a pre-tax yield of 5% is probably less attractive than a dividend from a Canadian corporation with a yield of 4%.

Interest Income, Dividend Income, and Capital Gains

Interest Income

Interest income typically comes from fixed income investments such as guaranteed investment certificates (GICs), bonds, treasury bills, banker's acceptance, commercial paper, promissory notes, and some mutual funds. When you purchase investments such as these, interest payments are made to you for the use of your monies. Tax on interest income is charged at the highest tax rate and is treated the same way as employment income. Interest income is fully added to your other sources of income including employment, pensions, rental income, dividends, and other types of regular income received.

Example:
> **GIC purchased for $20,000 at 5%**
> **Interest income earned in the year: $1,000**
> **Amount of taxes paid: $1,000 x 46% = $460**
> **Net return after taxes: $540**
> ***Assuming 46% marginal tax bracket**

Dividend Income

The dividend tax credit (DTC) is applied to both federal and provincial tax payable. The tax credit is used to recognize that a corporation paying a dividend has already paid tax on the earnings within the corporation that are now being distributed to the investors.

The tax payable on dividend income from Canadian corporations is first calculated by "grossing up" the actual dividends received by 45%. A tax credit is then applied in the amount of approximately 19% of the actual grossed-up amount to the net federal tax payable. Provincial tax is then calculated using the provincial tax rates and a provincial dividend tax credit rate.

Example:
    Dividend fund purchased for $20,000
    Dividends paid over a one-year period: $1,000
    Amount included in income: $1,000 x 1.45 = $1,450
    Personal income tax to be paid: $1,450 x 46% = $667
    Federal dividend tax credit: $1,450 x 19% = $276
    Amount of taxes paid: $667 - $276 = $391
    Net return after taxes: $609
    ***Assuming 46% marginal tax bracket**

As mentioned previously, it is important to consider the after-tax return on investments. However, this should not be the only factor in deciding what types of investments to select. You should also consider factors such as objectives, time horizon, and risk tolerance.

In trying to figure which investments provide a higher after-tax return based on your marginal tax rate, consider a factor between 1.23 and 1.32, which will vary based on marginal tax rates and your province of residency. This means that an investment providing you with interest income would have to pay approximately 28% more than a dividend yield for after-tax returns to be similar, assuming all other factors are equal.

Capital Gains
Capital gains result when the value of your investment has increased since it was purchased. Capital gains are realized when the investment is sold and there is a difference between

the purchase amount and the selling price. The cost of the investment is known as the adjusted cost base (ACB).

In terms of tax effectiveness, capital gains are treated most favourably when compared to interest and dividend income. The reason for the tax effectiveness is that only 50% of the gain is taxable. The other 50% of the capital gain is tax-free.

Example:
> **Index fund is purchased for $10,000 and thereafter sold for $11,000**
> **Capital gains earned: $1,000**
> **Amount of taxable capital gains: $1,000 x 50% = $500**
> **Amount of taxes paid: $500 x 46% = $230**
> **Net return after taxes: $760**
> ***Assuming 46% marginal tax bracket**

In addition to the favourable tax treatment, capital gains also provide investors with the potential added benefit of tax deferral. Interest income, whether received yearly or compounded, must be declared on a yearly basis. Dividends are typically paid out four times a year. Capital gains are only realized when an asset is sold. It is therefore possible to invest in an equity fund, stock, or other asset and not pay any tax when the asset is disposed of. Although capital gains are quite tax effective, you should understand what you are investing in, as certain types of investments that provide investors with potential capital gains can also hit them with capital losses. Also, some mutual funds, regardless of whether they are sold by the investor, can distribute capital gains at the end of the year.

Tax planning is important and you should obtain appropriate investment and taxation advice to ensure that effective strategies are put in place and that your investments are suitable in terms of matching your objectives, risk tolerance, and desired time horizon. It is important not to simply select investments that are treated favourably by the Canada Revenue Agency (CRA).

To clarify, many items are subject to capital gains tax if sold for a price higher than what you paid for them. Investments such as real estate, mutual funds, stocks, bonds, artwork, and other collectibles are subject to potential capital gains tax. The one exception to the taxation of capital gains is the profit realized on the sale of your principal residence.

In looking for investments that provide capital gains potential with little or no risk, talk to your advisor about the benefits of principal protected notes. These investments are fully guaranteed at maturity—some pay out distributions every year, while others do only at maturity. For example, if you select a note that is fully guaranteed at maturity and does not pay out any distributions until maturity, the growth would typically be classified as interest income if held to maturity. However, most of the time, these notes would trade in a secondary market and could be sold for a potential capital gain before maturity. Principal protected notes are offered by many financial planners and can be an important asset in your investment portfolio.

Alternative Minimum Tax (AMT)

Alternative Minimum Tax (AMT) ensures that high-income users cannot reduce their income by using tax deductions such as tax shelters to create a situation where little or no income tax is paid. AMT is an alternative to regular income tax whereby one must pay the higher of the two, but not both.

AMT adds back to standard taxable income the following for the purposes of calculating the adjusted taxable income:

- One quarter of net capital gains, which includes any capital gains an individual has claimed as a capital gains exemption;

- Net losses resulting from tax shelter investments and as a limited partner of a limited partnership;
- Net losses as a result of deductions of carrying charges on certain investments, including rental property, flow-through investments, and resource property;
- Net losses created by capital cost allowance claimed for certified films and certified productions; and
- Net losses resulting from resource expenditures and depletion allowances.

AMT should be a concern for those who have significant deductions from the above-mentioned factors. Individuals must calculate their taxable income using both methods: the regular method and the AMT method. The method that creates the higher tax payable is the one that must be used.

Chapter 2
Income Splitting

Family members generally use income splitting for reallocating income amongst the members to reduce the total amount of tax paid by the combined family unit. Income splitting is an acceptable method of reducing household taxes; however, some of these strategies are restricted by income attribution rules.

Income attribution rules are extremely important to take into consideration when implementing a financial and tax-reducing plan. Under these rules, income earned on capital that has been transferred either as a loan or gift to other family members may be attributed back and taxed in the hands of the individual who gifted the capital.

When planning to reduce taxable income with other family members, ensure to consult with a qualified and experienced tax specialist and/or financial planner. Although income-splitting rules restrict the number of ways currently available to split income, there are a number of effective ways it can be accomplished.

You can use income splitting with three distinct parties: your spouse, your children under eighteen years of age, and your children over eighteen years of age. Remember, the purpose of income splitting is to take income from a family member in a high tax bracket and shift the income to another member in a lower tax bracket. The result should be greater after-tax family income.

Income Splitting with Your Spouse

Spousal RRSPs

Income splitting strategies are generally implemented during working years, and proper planning will help families well into retirement with excellent results. An objective of income splitting is to ensure spouses have equal amounts of retirement income. This is accomplished by managing RRSP contributions to ensure equal levels of retirement income are received upon retirement.

For example, let's say an individual employed as a computer technician at a company and who earns about $60,000 is entitled to a company pension at retirement equivalent to about $30,000 per year and whose spouse earns $35,000 a year with no company pension plan. This family should take advantage of a spousal RRSP, whereby the higher-income earner contributes to a spousal RRSP. They take these tax deductions, and when they draw from the spousal RRSP at retirement, the income is taxed in the hands of the lower-income spouse. Attribution rules exist for spousal RRSP plans, meaning a higher-income spouse should not contribute to a spousal plan where withdrawals will be made by the lower-income spouse in the year the contributions were made or within the two proceeding years.

Invest the Earnings of the Lower-Income Spouse

If there is a desire to establish non-registered investment capital, you should keep the employment earnings of the lower-income spouse separate if possible. This allows the investment income earned to be taxed in the hands of the lower-income spouse. You should use the earnings of the higher-income spouse to cover all liabilities of the family, including mortgage payments, leasing payments, car payments, and other liabilities.

Pay Your Spouse a Salary

A business owner can pay their spouse a salary for any work the spouse performs. The amount of the salary must be a reasonable amount for the work provided. A business owner, for example, cannot pay their spouse $50,000 per year for stuffing some envelopes a few times a month.

Paying a spouse a salary will pass income from a high-income earner to someone in a lower tax bracket. This strategy also helps the spouse build RRSP contribution room and allows individuals to contribute to the Canada Pension Plan.

Income on Income

Attribution rules do not affect income that you receive on gifted or loaned capital. Although the income earned on the original capital is taxed back in the hands of the gifting person, the income earned thereafter on those funds is not. This method can result in substantial savings over a lengthy period of time.

For example, assume Mr. Jones gifts $200,000 to Mrs. Jones, who is the lower-income earner and a homemaker, and invests the money in an interest-bearing investment such as a corporate bond or private mortgage at 10% per year. Each year, $20,000 is taxed in the hands of Mr. Jones. After the first year, however, the interest on the $20,000 is taxed in the hands of Mrs. Jones.

Loans to a Spouse Used to Finance a Business

Business income is not attributable back to the gifting spouse. Therefore, any business income earned will be taxed in the business owner's hands.

Income Splitting with Your Children

Income Splitting with Your Children under Age Eighteen

Income earned on capital transferred to a child under the age of eighteen as either a gift or loan is attributed back to the transferring family member except for capital gains and losses. Other than shelters such as Registered Education Savings Plans (RESPs), there are very few income splitting strategies that can be used with children. The Canada Child Tax Benefit (CCTB) can be given to the child whereby the payments are taxed in the hands of the child even if the income earned is interest income.

Income Splitting with Your Children Eighteen Years of Age and Over

Income earned on capital gifted to adult children is not attributed back to the gift giver. Once you transfer capital to adult children, income splitting is achieved. Your adult children, however, will then own the assets and are free to do what they wish with them.

Pension Income Splitting for Seniors

Individuals are able to allocate up to 50% of income to a spouse or common-law partner if the income qualifies for the pension tax credit. This means that couples have the opportunity to pay less income tax, since certain types of pension income, including RRIF income, can be split amongst partners. Income that qualifies for pension splitting depends on the individual's age and is split as follows:

Recipients age sixty-five or over:
- Income from an RRSP, which is annuitized
- Registered Retirement Income Fund (RRIF), Life Income Fund (LIF), and Locked-In RIF withdrawals
- Income from annuitized deferred profit-sharing plans
- Pension income from a Registered Pension Plan (RPP)

Recipients under the age of sixty-five:
- Pension income from an RPP, which can be either a defined benefit plan or a defined contribution plan

Income that cannot be split between spouses or common-law partners includes:

- RRSP withdrawals
- Canada Pension Plan (CPP)*
- Quebec Pension Plan (QPP)
- Old Age Security (OAS)
- Guaranteed Income Supplement (GIS)
- Retirement Compensation Arrangements (RCAs)
- RRSP annuities for those under the age of sixty-five
- RRIF annuities for those under the age of sixty-five
- Deferred Profit Sharing Plan (DPSP) annuities for those under the age of sixty-five

*Canada Pension Plan (CPP) income does not qualify as eligible income for either the pension income credit or pension splitting; however, CPP retirement benefits can be split. Spouses and common-law partners can split CPP income under a formula that takes into consideration the number of years married or living together during the period they were required to contribute to the plan.

Chapter 3

Registered Retirement Savings Plans (RRSPs)

Canada's most popular tax shelter is the Registered Retirement Savings Plan. The 2007 maximum allowable RRSP contribution for individuals who do not participate in a registered pension plan is 18% of an individual's earned income to a maximum of $19,000. The maximum limit is $20,000 for 2008, $21,000 for 2009, and $22,000 for 2010.

For members of registered pension plans or deferred profit-sharing plans, the maximum allowable RRSP contribution is equal to the maximum limit or 18% of an individual's earned income, whichever is lower, minus an amount that totals both the employee and employer contributions to a registered pension plan. The total employee and employer contributions are known as the pension adjustment.

Let's look at an example. Sofia earns $80,000 per year and contributes $2,200 to her registered pension plan at work. Her employer contributes $3,700 to her plan as well.
Sofia's maximum allowable contribution is calculated as follows:

- $80,000 x 18% = $9,600
- The maximum allowable contribution is $9,600 minus the pension adjustment of $2,200 plus $3,700. Therefore, Sofia's maximum allowable RRSP contribution is $3,900 [$9,600 minus ($2,200 + $3,700)]. The amount of the

contribution is then deducted from her taxable income, thereby providing immediate tax relief.

RRSP contribution limits are based on a percentage of earned income. Earned income includes income from the following sources:
- Salaries or wages minus any allowable deductions
- Income from a business, either a sole proprietorship or a partnership
- Income from royalties for things including inventions and authored works
- Disability pensions from both Canada Pension Pensions and Quebec Pension Plans, assuming residency in Canada when the payments were made
- Real estate net rental income
- Taxable net research grants
- Alimony and maintenance payments
- Supplementary unemployment benefit plan payments

The following is subtracted:
- Losses from businesses either as a sole proprietor or as a partner (must be actively involved)
- Net rental losses
- Alimony or maintenance payments that are deductible
- Negative cumulative capital losses that are eligible and have been included in business income

The deadline for contributing to a RRSP for the previous tax year is sixty days from the beginning of the year.

An RRSP is simply a tax shelter that defers income to a later point in one's life. The contributions to the tax shelter and the interest and/or growth in the plan are not taxed until the funds are withdrawn.

Let's assume that you invested $10,000 each year at the beginning of the year into an RRSP for a period of twenty-five years in an RRSP than was earning 8% per year. At the end of twenty-five years, you would have $789,544. Assuming you are in a 40% marginal tax rate, you would have also saved approximately $4,000 per year in income tax because of the contributions.

Now let's assume instead of investing $10,000 each year into an RRSP, you decided to invest the same amount in a non-registered investment account earning 8% per year for a period of twenty-five years and paid the income tax on the earnings every year. Assuming a 40% marginal tax rate and that the investment income was interest income, you would have approximately $486,607 in non-registered funds. This is a difference of $302,937. The numbers look even better if we took the $4,000 a year in tax savings and invested them.

If we assume you invested the $4,000 every year for twenty-four years as a $10,000 investment into an RRSP today, it will generate the equivalent in tax refunds of about $4,000 next year. The investment portfolio at the end of the period would be worth about $267,059. This is assuming no tax was payable on the growth of the investment over the twenty-four-year period, which is possible if investments such as corporate class funds are used.

Proper planning using an RRSP would provide you with an income flow from your RRSP funds over many years while sheltering the income earned from tax during the years the funds are in the registered plan.

You should consider other strategies when using an RRSP to reduce your immediate tax burden and to generate the best possible earnings inside and outside of your registered plans:

• *Contribute as early as possible in the year or set a monthly purchase plan.* Although many people wait until the RRSP deadline to max-out their contributions, contribute at the beginning of the year or set up a monthly purchase plan to attain a tax advantage of further compounding benefits and possibly the benefits of dollar cost averaging if you use mutual funds.

- *Contribute in low-income years and save the tax deduction for a following year when your income will be higher.* Let's assume you are in a low-income tax bracket because you decided to travel for a while, went back to school, or took some time off to spend with your family. Consider contributing to an RRSP to take advantage of the benefits of compounding. However, claim the deduction when your income level increases and you are in a higher marginal tax bracket.

- *Transfer your retiring allowance or severance pay into an RRSP.* Certain limitations exist, but consider transferring your retiring allowance or severance pay into an RRSP when you retire or when you leave your employer. Sick benefits, severance pay, and retiring allowances can provide you with immediate tax relief if transferred to your RRSP.

- *Structure your registered and non-registered investments so that your interest-bearing investments are in your RRSP account.* Assuming your investment objectives, time horizon, and risk tolerance are the same or similar for both types of investment portfolios, consider holding investments such as bonds, GICs, and other interest-bearing investments in your registered portfolio. Hold investments that earn capital gains and dividends, such as stocks and growth mutual funds, outside of registered portfolios. By structuring your investments like this, you reduce your exposure to tax.

Consider the following example. Mr. Follett has an RRSP worth approximately $100,000. He also has a non-registered portfolio worth $100,000. Mr. Follett will not need access to any of the funds for at least ten to fifteen years. He is an investor with an average amount of investment knowledge and is willing to take a certain amount of risk in his overall investments. Mr. Follett is comfortable with a balanced portfolio and currently holds a balanced fund for both of his investments. He figures he is a balanced investor, so this is the appropriate asset mix, which typically is a 50/50 split between equities and fixed-income investments.

Although the asset mix might be correct based on all of the combined assets, it should not be the same between the RRSP and non-registered portfolios. Mr. Follett has a combined $200,000 in registered and non-registered investments. With a 50/50 split, he should hold approximately $100,000 in fixed-income investments and $100,000 in growth-oriented investments. A more tax-effective way of maintaining the same balance between equities and fixed income would be to simply hold his fixed-income investments in his RRSP account and to hold his growth-oriented investments outside his RRSP account to take advantage of potential capital gains or capital losses. Therefore, instead of holding a balanced fund for both accounts, he should hold investments comprised possibly of bonds, bond and income funds, and other interest-bearing investments inside the RRSP account. Investments such as growth equity funds, stocks, dividend funds, and dividend paying preferred shares and common shares should be held outside of his RRSP account.

Other strategies include:

- *Name your spouse as a beneficiary to your RRSP.* The entire amount of your accumulated RRSP account is added to your income upon death unless you have named your spouse or dependent child as a beneficiary. Your spouse would be able to roll the funds in your RRSP account over to their RRSP account without incurring any income tax. It is extremely important to consider the impact of taxes on one's registered plans upon death.

    For example, Mr. Garaci is widowed and has an RRSP valued at $500,000. He has named one of his children as the beneficiary to his RRSP because his other child is receiving the non-registered monies he has accumulated in a bank account and GIC investment with his bank, totalling $500,000. With this setup, his one child would receive the $500,000 RRSP and his estate would in essence be taxed because the $500,000 would be added to his taxable income because the children were not dependents. Assuming a 50% tax bracket, $250,000 in taxes would have to be paid and would be taken from the monies outside of the registered plans.

The end result is one child being left with $500,000 and the other being left with $250,000 after paying the government the $250,000 in taxes. In reality, some siblings would probably come to a compromise and split the estate equally in half. However, by law, they would not have to if you structured your will this way.

- *Contribute to a spousal RRSP*. If your spouse is expected to have a lower amount of retirement income than you, consider the benefits of spousal RRSPs. Any amount an individual is allowed to contribute to their RRSP may be contributed to a spousal RRSP. You still get the deduction, but at retirement, your spouse will be in a lower tax bracket and pay tax at lower rates than you.
- *Retiring outside of Canada*. A small percentage of individuals leave Canada at retirement. When you leave the country, you are not required to collapse your RRSP. Under normal conditions, when Canadians withdraw money from their RRSP, they are taxed at a high tax rate when all income is combined. Individuals retiring outside of Canada might consider the benefits of becoming a non-resident. By becoming a non-resident, you would pay a maximum amount of withholding tax of 25%. The figure can be considerably less depending on the country where you take residency and the existing tax treaty Canada has with that country.

Married or common-law partners should consider the benefits of spousal RRSPs in certain situations. You should consider a spousal RRSP when one person is in a higher tax bracket, and you should use it as a tool to split income at retirement.

The following situation demonstrates why you should consider a spousal plan. Mr. Jones is a high-school teacher who, at the age of sixty-five, will be entitled to a pension from work in the amount of $40,000 per year. This pension income is derived from his employer registered pension plan, which is funded by both the employee and the employer. Because of the contributions to the pension plan, Mr. Jones' yearly RRSP contributions are limited to approximately $3,000 per year. Mrs. Jones is self-employed and does not have a company pension plan. Her earned income is approximately $25,000 per year and she contributed 18% of her earnings to her RRSP.

Under this example, it would make more sense if Mr. Jones contributed the $3,000 per year into his wife's spousal RRSP account. When the funds are withdrawn, let's say, for example, in twenty years, the income is attributed to Mrs. Jones. However, the contributions were deducted by Mr. Jones from his earned income.

With regards to spousal RRSPs, a few additional factors need to be considered. If a withdrawal is made by the non-contributing spouse in the same year or in the two proceeding calendar years after a spousal contribution is made, the income will be attributed back to the contributing spouse.

For example, if Mr. Jones contributes to his wife's spousal RRSP in December 2007, and if his wife withdraws funds prior to January 1, 2010, the income would be attributed back to Mr. Jones. If the spousal contribution was made on January 2, 2008, any funds withdrawn from Mrs. Jones' spousal RRSP before January 1, 2011 would be attributed back to Mr. Jones.

With spousal RRSPs, it is also possible for a spouse over the age of seventy-one with earned income to contribute to a spousal RRSP if the receiving spouse is under the age of seventy-one.

The Carry-Forward Rule

If you do not contribute the maximum allowable amount in any given year, you can carry forward the unused RRSP deduction room indefinitely.

Consider the following:
- Unused contribution room is not lost and may be carried forward.
- Consider making contributions in lower-income years and not deducting them against income until in a higher tax bracket.
- Take advantage of the benefits of spousal RRSPs.
- Hold interest-bearing investments inside RRSPs and investments which pay dividends and potential capital gains outside of RRSPs.
- Start contributing early and maximize the benefits of compound interest.
- Spousal RRSP contributions can be made in years after the contributing individual is over the age of sixty-nine if earned income exists.

Chapter 4
Flow-Through Investments

Flow-Through Shares and Limited Partnerships
Over the past several years, the Department of Finance has eliminated many loopholes that taxpayers have been exploiting to defer or save taxes. Investing in flow-through shares and flow-through limited partnerships can be an important tool in tax planning for Canadians. If your financial advisor or financial institution does not offer flow-through shares or flow-through limited partnerships, you might be missing a huge opportunity to reduce your tax liability.

Flow-through shares and limited partnerships have been included in the Income Tax Act to provide resource companies with an attractive method of raising funds for resource exploration and other development activities. Without getting into specific details about how the Canadian Exploration Expenses (CEE), Canadian Development Expenses (CDE) or Canadian Renewable and Conservation Expenses (CRCE) work in Canada, I will briefly explain how flow-throughs can reduce your tax liability.

Tax Benefits
Flow-through shares offer immediate and direct tax benefits. The benefits are based on two factors: tax savings and tax deferral.

Investors usually receive a full deduction equal to their investments. In other words, an investment is fully deductible against any source of income. The immediate tax savings for the investor will result in the individual incurring a low adjusted cost base for the flow-through investment. Therefore, when the flow-through shares are sold, the proceeds of the disposition are taxed as capital gains. Capital gains are taxed at half the rate of ordinary income and this differential generates potential tax savings. In addition to the immediate tax savings, the investment also provides the potential for attractive investment returns.

Deferring the disposition of flow-through shares to subsequent years defers the tax liability on disposition. Most flow-through investments have to be held for a period of between eighteen months and three years. Ask your financial advisor for specific details.

Although capital gains tax does have to be paid at disposition, investors benefit from tax deferral and the time value of money. Investors receive enhanced tax benefits where they have net capital losses carried forward to offset the capital gains from the disposition of the flow-through shares.

For example, lets assume you had invested $12,000 in Nortel Networks when the shares where trading at $122. You had subsequently sold them when they dropped in value and were left with $2,000. You had incurred a $10,000 capital loss, which you can carry forward indefinitely. You then invested $10,000 into a flow-through share, wishing to reduce your taxable income in 2006. In 2008, let's assume the $10,000 investment is still worth $10,000. On disposition, you would incur a $10,000 capital gain. However, this amount can be reduced to zero based on your previous $10,000 capital loss. Also, many flow-through limited partnerships allow you to roll your flow-through investment into a mutual fund, thereby delaying your capital gains even further.

The bottom line is that many individuals can benefit from flow-through investments. Deal with an institution that can at least offer them to you to ensure you are receiving unbiased advice. They may not make sense for you, but make sure they don't make sense because of your personal situation and not because your banker or your advisor does not offer them.

Flow-through shares are generally acquired through a limited partnership. The limited partnership similar to a mutual fund provides added diversification and therefore reduces risk. Similar to mutual funds, an investor purchases units of the fund, which in turn invests the funds in flow-through shares of selected companies.

Although you can use flow-through limited partnerships to reduce taxable income, other benefits include:

- *Avoiding Old Age Security (OAS) clawbacks.* OAS benefits begin to be reduced when taxable income reaches $63,511 for the year 2007. The OAS repayment is 15% of the excess income over $63,511 to a maximum amount of the OAS received. If a taxpayer's income is $102,865, the OAS benefit is fully repaid. A senior investor with a taxable income of $100,000 who makes a $40,000 investment into a flow-through share or limited partnership may receive a couple of immediate benefits:

  1. Additional current-year tax reductions of approximately $18,000; and
  2. Full restoration of Old Age Security benefits.

- *Reducing source deductions.* Individuals may also consider flow-through securities if they would like to reduce source deductions from their current employer. Self-employed individuals may reduce or possibly eliminate quarterly tax installment payments.

- *Managing registered plans including RRSPs, LIFs, and RIFs.* Unlocking your registered plans is possible by using flow-through shares. Some individuals have accumulated significant funds in their registered plans by a variety of ways that may include maximum contributions, severance packages, solid returns, and pension transfers. Income from registered plans is fully taxable at an individual's marginal tax rate.

Whether you wish to reduce your taxable income or whether you are looking to reduce the size of registered assets, you can use flow-through shares to reduce the immediate tax liability. For example, if you are taking an annuity payment or RIF payment from your registered plan and you do not require the income, it can be invested in flow-through shares to offset the taxes while still holding an asset with value. Since the value of the flow-through share or limited partnership could decline, you should consider this strategy in relation to your overall risk tolerance and objectives.

- *Sheltering lump sums of income from taxes.* Some investors receive a large sum as income in one particular year. This income could be a result of the sale of a cottage that has accrued substantial capital gains, the sale of a stock that has significantly appreciated, or even the sale of a business. In these situations, investors can purchase flow-through shares or limited partnership fund units to reduce the immediate tax liability and defer the liability to future years when their income might be at a lower marginal tax rate.

- *Ownership of limited partnership units by corporations.* Corporations can invest in flow-through shares or limited partnerships. If a corporation has capital-loss carry-forwards, the disposition of the flow-through investment will partially or fully offset previous capital losses. If there are no previous capital losses, the disposition of units generating a capital gain will increase the corporation's capital dividend account. The increase in the capital dividend account will be equal to the 50% non-taxable capital gain. If at any point there is a positive balance in the capital dividend account, the corporation can pay a tax-free dividend to its shareholders.

Chapter 5
Super Flow-Through Investments

Super flow-through investments provide additional tax incentives for investors. With flow-through shares, investors typically have a 100% deduction against income. With super flow-through investments, investors receive an additional 15% non-refundable tax credit. This tax credit is applicable to eligible "grassroots" explorations in Canada and is deducted from federal income tax payable. In addition, provincial and territorial tax credits exist and vary from province to province.

The tax credits are in addition to the 100% deduction allowed with regular flow-through investments. The additional tax credits mean that for those individuals in the highest marginal tax brackets, the added 15% non-refundable tax credit leads to an exploration expense deduction equivalent to over 135% for federal tax purposes.

The federal tax credit is a non-fundable tax credit. This means that you have to pay tax to be able to benefit. You can carry back the credit and apply it against taxes paid in the previous three years, and you may carry forward unused credits for up to ten years.

The super flow-through program is actually called Canada's Mineral Exploration Tax Credit. The program was introduced in October 2000 as a tax incentive for grassroots mineral exploration. The program was originally intended to be three years in length, as it was implemented as a short-term measure to help Canada's mineral exploration problems from the '90s. The program has been extended twice since inception, and both extensions were for one-year periods. The program has currently been extended to March 31, 2008.

Flow-through investments and super flow-through investments are available through licensed advisors. For example, in the province of Ontario, super flow-through limited partnerships are only available through the member firms of the Investment Dealers Association (IDA) and some members of the Mutual Fund Dealers Association (MFDA) who are also licensed as Limited Market Dealers. Ask your advisor if they are licensed to provide you with advice on flow-through investments.

Chapter 6

Corporate Class Funds

Corporate class mutual funds are very tax efficient investments for two reasons: 1) they offer tax deferral until the investment is actually sold, and 2) the income paid out is in the form of a capital gain.

There are currently about a dozen or so mutual fund companies that offer corporate class funds, and many of these funds are available through most independent financial planning and investment organizations. It is important that your financial advisor be familiar with the benefits of corporate class mutual funds and able to offer them if they would benefit you.

Corporate class funds are established as mutual fund corporations rather than mutual fund trusts. They are set up with multiple share classes, each of which is a different fund. Because of the share and corporate structure, investors can buy into the different classes of shares within the corporation and buy and sell without triggering any capital gains. They therefore work in a similar way as an RRSP in that the investment is only taxed when it is withdrawn from the corporation. However, unlike RRSPs, where the withdrawn amount is treated as income, with corporate class funds, the growth of the investment is turned into a capital gain. Income is normally taxed if it is generated from bonds or other fixed income investments.

Features of Corporate Class Funds

- Investors may switch between corporate class funds without triggering capital gains or losses.
- Capital gains or losses are only triggered when investors redeem from the corporation.
- Investors benefit from tax deferral as capital gains are paid on the redemption.
- Interest income typically from fixed income funds including money market funds and bond funds can be converted to tax efficient capital gains.
- Investment selection is available from over a dozen mutual fund companies that offer corporate class funds.
- Annual distributions from corporate class funds are minimized and, in and some cases, eliminated.
- Investment decisions can be made without being effected by tax concerns.
- Minimizing taxes is possible by ensuring capital gains and losses are triggered at the most advantageous time.

Let's look at an example of how corporate class funds can help grow your non-registered funds in a more tax efficient way. Mr. Damaso is in a 45% marginal tax bracket. He is looking to invest $50,000 and assumes an 8% rate of return for a thirty-year period. Mr. Damaso is an investor who will rebalance his account annually. The return outside a corporate class structure would be taxed annually.

After thirty years with a regular mutual fund, Mr. Damaso would have an investment portfolio valued at $321,530. If he invested in a corporate class mutual fund structure, his portfolio would be worth $503,500 with an after-tax value of $412,500. The corporate class structure provides Mr. Damaso with $90,000 in additional funds over the same period.

The benefit is that all three types of investment income, interest, dividends, and capital gains, are all treated as capital gains on the redemption from the corporate class structure. The power of compounding and tax deferral is significant to provide investors with substantial tax savings resulting in greater accumulated wealth.

After-Tax Returns

	Gross	Tax	After Tax
Interest Income	5%	2.5%	2.5%
Capital Gains	5%	1.25%	3.75%
		Plus	50%

*assumes 46.41% marginal tax rate

Corporate class funds are ideal for investors who have maximized their RRSPs and have taken advantage of other tax reduction strategies including investments such as flow-through shares. In addition, they are good investments for individuals

- with limited RRSP contribution room because of company pension plans;
- who split income with minor children without triggering income attribution rules;
- with funds outside of registered plans;
- with funds outside of registered plans who invest into fixed income mutual funds;
- who rebalance their portfolios on a regular basis;
- who wish to control when capital gains or losses are triggered; and/or
- who wish to grow their portfolios through deferral of capital gains tax.

Using Corporate Class Funds to Split Income with Children

Income splitting with minor children triggers income attribution back to the transferor of funds unless the income is in the form of a capital gain. By using corporate class funds, capital gain income will result in greater tax efficiency for the whole family. The child's account will benefit from tax-efficient growth and possibly tax-free growth, assuming no other income exists for the child.

Chapter 7
ROC Funds

Return of capital (ROC) funds are available through some mutual fund companies and provide investors with a relatively higher level of stable tax-efficient cash flow. With regular mutual funds, investors might receive income and capital gains on a yearly basis and are therefore income taxable in the year they were received, whereas ROC funds provide investors with cash flow that is non-taxable in the year it is received.

In essence, ROC is the portion of the cash flow or distribution that actually exceeds the net income and net capital gains of the fund. The distribution itself represents a portion of invested capital and is therefore not taxable in the year you receive the income. Since the distributions are non-taxable in the year received, the adjusted cost base (ACB) of the units held will decrease, resulting in a capital gain in the future.

Systematic withdrawal plans (SWPs) are sometimes confused with ROC funds. SWPs provide individuals with a series of withdrawals, usually on a monthly basis. The withdrawals occur by selling units at regular intervals.

ROC funds can provide benefits over SWPs, which can include:
- Potential increase of monthly cash flow;
- Cash flow that is more predictable than regular mutual funds;

- Potential to lower an investor's marginal tax rate in the year an ROC distribution is made;
- Flexibility to decide when to incur a tax liability in some situations; and
- The potential to pay less income tax if your tax rate is lowered in future years.

Let's look at the following scenario to see how ROC funds work. Lisa is a senior and has $150,000 in a non-registered investment account. We will assume an 8% target distribution rate. Lisa will receive $1,000 per month.

When selecting ROC funds, many types are available and they typically range in annual distributions from 4% to 8%. Lisa's adjusted cost base (ACB) will be decreased year over year because the annual distribution is a combination of return of capital and income. When her ACB reaches zero, any future ROC distributions are treated as realized capital gains in the year the payments are received.

It is important to note that the distribution is not the actual rate of return and that the rate of return can be either lesser or greater than the actual distribution. If, for example, you select a fund with a target distribution of 6% and the fund actually earned 7%, the market value of the investment will increase over time. In this situation, you will receive the 6% distribution from the investment and the ACB will fall to zero at around year fifteen, and then any future distributions will be taxed as capital gains. Remember, just because the ACB has fallen to zero, it doesn't mean that the value of the investment has dropped to zero. The market value would actually be higher than the original invested amount.

When the return on the ROC fund is actually lower than the distribution, the market value of the investment drops as you receive your return of capital distributions. If, for example, the return on a ROC fund is 5% and the target distribution is 6% per annum, your ACB would fall to zero around year eighteen due to the distributions being reset lower each year in this situation.

ROC funds can provide you with many benefits and you should ensure your advisor is familiar with the many ROC funds offered in the marketplace. ROC funds are available through a number of mutual fund companies, including Fidelity, Mackenzie, AGF, and a few others.

Chapter 8
Labour-Sponsored Investment Funds

Labour-sponsored investment funds (LSIFs) are venture capital funds that invest in smaller, less established private companies with some strong growth potential. These up-and-coming companies can be in a wide variety of sectors, including biotechnology, information technology, financial services, energy, and many others.

An LSIF investment can be classified as a high-risk investment if viewed on its own. However, if used properly, LSIFs are an ideal way for investors to reduce risk, enhance returns, and generate tax credits and tax refunds.

Labour-sponsored investment funds will hold many positions in companies comprising the fund, making them similar to mutual funds, and therefore reducing the overall investment risk. Investors provide the capital needed for small- and medium-sized businesses to realize their maximum potential. In return, investors are allowed to participate in the great potential of the venture capital market while minimizing the risks involved in venture capital investing by benefiting from the knowledge and expertise of the many different venture capital investment teams. The most important aspect, however, is that the federal and provincial governments provide generous tax breaks for investors of these funds.

Benefits

You can invest in a labour-sponsored fund both inside and outside of registered plans. Most investors have traditionally invested in LSIFs inside of registered plans because they receive the benefits of investing in RRSPs, allowing them to receive the double benefit of federal and provincial tax credits.

Investing inside of an RRSP can provide investors with two key benefits that mutual funds do not offer:

1. Up to 35% in tax credits, which include a 15% federal tax credit and a 20% provincial tax credit on the amount invested to a maximum of $5,000 with a minimum investment of $500. This is in addition to the RRSP contribution tax benefits. The majority of LSIFs provide investors with a combined 30% tax credit. The 35% tax credit is available for funds whose holdings in Canadian companies are more heavily research oriented. The companies in which the fund invests are typically further away from generating revenues and are therefore considered more speculative in nature. These funds are known as research-oriented investment funds.

2. There is potential for long-term above-average returns, since most of an LSIF is invested in private companies in the early stages of their development.

The maximum tax credit is therefore $1,750 on a $5,000 investment. As with many mutual funds, investors typically purchase these funds on a back-end load or deferred sales charge. This should not factor into your decision on whether LSIFs are suitable investments for your particular needs, as you must hold these funds for eight years or you must repay the tax credits.

The Ontario government announced plans to phase out the 15% tax credit for investors in LSIFs by the end of the

2010 taxation year.

LSIFs have lost popularity over the last decade, as the returns on the majority of the funds have been lackluster. In addition, many investors and advisors have stayed away from these funds because the underlying management fees are substantially higher than those of regular mutual funds. However, for those unconcerned with the slightly higher management fees, the tax credits alone with the added diversification provide added financial benefits to portfolios. Best Funds provides access to LSIFs that offer Ontario investors both the 30% and 35% tax credit. The B.E.S.T. Discoveries Fund and Axis Investment Fund are well-known kinds in the LSIF spectrum.

Tax Savings for Labour-Sponsored Investments—Ontario

Taxable Income[1,4]	Investment[2]	RRSP Tax Savings[4]	30% Tax Credit[3,6]	Total Tax Savings[4,5]	After-Tax Cost[4]
Up to $35,488	$5,000	up to $1,078	$1,500	up to $2,578	at least $2,422
$35,488 to $37,178	$5,000	$1,233	$1,500	$2,733	$2,267
$37,179 to $62,487	$5,000	$1,558	$1,500	$3,058	$1,942
$62,488 to $70,976	$5,000	$1,649	$1,500	$3,149	$1,851
$70,977 to $73,622	$5,000	$1,770	$1,500	$3,270	$1,730
$73,623 to $74,357	$5,000	$1,971	$1,500	$3,471	$1,529
$74,358 to $120,887	$5,000	$2,171	$1,500	$3,671	$1,329
$120,888 and over	$5,000	$2,321	$1,500	$3,821	$1,179

Notes:

1. Taxable income is gross income less income tax deductions allowed by the Federal Tax Act and the Ontario Tax Act. The brackets starting at $62,487 and $73,622 relate to provincial surtaxes and assume that only the basic personal credit is available under the Ontario Tax Act.

2. The RRSP contribution assumes that the investor is within their contribution limit and can deduct the entire contribution.

3. The Federal Credits and Ontario Credits are generally avail-

able if the investor has tax otherwise payable against which to offset the tax credits. Maximum tax credits apply in respect of all purchases of shares of prescribed labour-sponsored venture capital corporations or labour-sponsored investment fund corporations.

4.　The income tax rates are based on the federal and Ontario income tax legislation as of January 1, 2007 and any proposals to amend such legislation announced before that date. They are the 2007 marginal tax rates for investment income other than capital gains and dividends for individuals residing in Ontario.

5.　Additional tax savings result from the RRSP deduction reducing taxable income and are calculated at the marginal income tax rates. RRSP tax savings are not unique to labour-sponsored investment funds and are available on any RRSP eligible investment, provided that the investment is within contribution limits. Income taxes are paid on the withdrawal of funds from RRSPs.

6.　Repayment of the Federal Credits and Ontario Credits might be required if the shares are redeemed within eights years from the date of purchase.

It is important to note that you will have to pay back your tax credits if the investment is sold prior to the eighth anniversary of the date of purchase.

　　One thing many individuals don't understand is that the investment into the LSIF does not have to be made with new money. It can be made with existing assets held in either your RRSP or non-registered investments.

Chapter 9

Index Funds and Exchange-Traded Funds (ETFs)

Index Funds

Index funds are managed on a passive basis and are comprised of investments that mirror the actual index from which they are derived. As an example, a Canadian index fund may hold the 300 stocks that compose the TSE300 Index.

Index funds became popular in the late '90s as investors started becoming conscious of the fact that index funds had lower management expense ratios (MERs) than regular mutual funds. In addition to the lower MERs, index funds also provide investors with a couple other benefits:

- *Performance*. Many individuals and experts believe that the majority of money managers underperform the index over the long term. Index funds may actually increase returns with lower associated management fees. However, even with index funds, it is important to diversify. Typically, investors should hold about 15% to 25% of their investments in index funds and index-related products.
- *Tax Benefits*. Index funds should provide investors with higher after-tax returns than actively managed mutual funds would. This is because index funds are managed on a passive basis, while regular mutual funds are managed actively and therefore undergo a greater number of trades. A greater number of trades will probably result in a greater capital gain distribution at the end of the year.

Tax efficiency and the amount of funds compounding over time are key factors in generating long-term excess returns. In most cases, index funds are more tax efficient than mutual funds and are close to fully invested into the markets. This means that index funds will have about 98% or more of their funds invested into the index, whereas some actively managed funds can be sitting with 4% to 10% in cash at any time. Index funds can provide added benefits to a well-balanced diversified portfolio, but by no means should an investor have a portfolio that is composed solely of index funds and index-related products.

Exchange-Traded Funds (ETFs)

Exchange-traded funds (ETFs) are a unique type of index fund. Index funds trade like regular mutual funds. If an investor buys a fund on Monday during the day, they would get the closing price on Monday and in essence won't know what the price is until the next day. ETFs in particular provide investors with added flexibility and some added benefits. ETFs trade like individual stocks. This means you can buy and sell them in any number of shares during regular market hours. You can also set prices on their orders, which are known as limit orders.

Although ETFs are more flexible than traditional index funds, I don't typically view this as an added benefit. However, ETFs will definitely provide investors with added tax efficiency greater than that of regular mutual funds and index funds. When any investor sells their index fund holdings, the manager has to sell holdings to fulfill the cash needs. If the selling of shares generates capital gains, those gains are passed on to all the remaining investors regardless of the fund's performance. ETFs do not work in the same way as index funds. They are bought and sold on an exchange, so regardless of how many other investors are buying or selling their shares, their trades will not affect your tax situation. In addition, ETFs can have capital gains distributions like index funds; however, these gains are not created by other investors.

Chapter 10

Structured Notes

Principal-protected notes (PPNs) are classified as structured notes. They are part of the structured product family, which are hybrid securities combining a fixed-income instrument with a series of derivative components. PPNs provide exposure to a variety of different markets while looking for innovative ways to guarantee your principal. These products satisfy risk-adverse investors who want to participate in the performance of assets such as equities, currencies, interest rates, or commodities but are unwilling to take the risk of absolute declines in their invested capital. PPNs provide the benefit of guaranteed capital, such as GICs and bonds, with the upside potential of higher-risk investments.

PPNs will typically have maturity terms ranging from five to ten years. Some issues offer shorter-term notes in the range of three to five years. Some mutual fund companies such as Franklin Templeton, Mackenzie, AIM Trimark, and CI have come out with versions of protected notes where they link the performance to some of their selected mutual funds. Other companies are creating links to hedge products as opposed to mainstream mutual funds. Semi-annual and annual income is possible with some issuers of protected notes. Other issuers provide investors with capital gains potential, tax deferral, and tax minimization, as any realized gains are in the year of maturity or disposition.

Whatever the case, the key is that these products provide a guarantee of capital with the potential for higher returns by linking the performance to equity type instruments. You can find a listing of currently available PPNs at www.guaranteedinvestments.com.

It is important to note that PPNs are not available through all financial advisors.

Chapter 11

Segregated Funds

Segregated funds are sometimes also known as guaranteed investment funds. These are common names given to individual variable insurance contracts. Segregated funds were typically considered appropriate investments for a small portion of the population, including business owners and professionals. Since segregated funds offer a number of attractive features and benefits, more investors today have taken advantage of these investments. They can provide individuals with principal guarantees at maturity or death or are useful to those looking for potential creditor protection.

Segregated funds are definitely not suitable for everyone. However, if you are looking for investments that provide the growth potential of mutual funds combined with the security of principal guarantees, then they might be appropriate for you. You should know that the added benefits of segregated funds come with a price: Segregated fund fees are higher than mutual fund fees.

Many insurance companies offer segregated funds. Product features vary, but since they are insurance products, segregated funds come with certain guarantees. The first guarantee is a death-benefit guarantee and the second is a deposit-maturity guarantee.

At death, the named beneficiary will receive the proceeds of the individual contract. The proceeds will be either the market value of the investment or the guaranteed amount stated in the contract, whichever is greater.

A deposit-maturity guarantee usually comes into effect a minimum of ten years from the date of your investment or deposit into the segregated fund. When the funds mature at this time, the guaranteed amount or the market value of the investment is paid out, whichever is greater. These guarantees typically range from 75% to 100% depending on the segregated fund purchased.

In addition to benefit guarantees on maturity and death, segregated funds provide investors the ability to reset their investments. This is typically known as a reset feature. Investors can trigger a reset feature when the market value of their investment is in excess of the original value. This provides investment gains by resetting the guaranteed value. The resetting feature will also affect the maturity date because a new maturity date is established when the reset is triggered. Reset features are different from company to company and need to be examined carefully. Some insurance providers also offer automatic reset features. A reset does not trigger capital gains.

Another important feature of segregated funds is the potential to creditor-proof your assets. For business owners and self-employed professionals, including doctors and dentists, it might be important to protect assets in cases of litigation or bankruptcy. Segregated funds are insurance contracts governed by insurance legislation and they offer the possibility of creditor protection that some other investments may not.

Probate fees are sometimes known as death taxes. One of the main features of segregated funds is they provide individuals with the ability to bypass probate. Probate is the process whereby a court approves a will as valid and the last testament of the deceased. The probate process is not only time consuming and complex, it also is costly. By naming a beneficiary on your segregated funds, the proceeds will bypass the probate process. Probate fees in Canada can be found in chapter 27, which deals with probate and estate taxes.

Chapter 12

Prescribed Annuities

An annuity is purchased through an insurance company. A life-insurance licensed broker must sell the annuity, which means that not many advisors offer them. With annuities, you invest monies with an insurance company, and in return, the insurance company makes regular income payments back to you. The income payments contain both interest and principal and can provide several options for payment guarantees.

Annuities can have many features, including:

- Income payments for a set period (typically three or more years);
- Guaranteed retirement income for life;
- Indexing of payments;
- Single life annuity (payments for life);
- Joint and last survivor annuity;
- Monthly, quarterly, semi-annual, or annual payments; and
- Income deferral.

Your annuity income is determined by a variety of factors at the time of the investment. The payout will depend on:

- The amount of funds invested;
- The length of time that annuity payments are to be guaranteed;
- The type of annuity;
- The interest rates at the time of investment;

- Your age; and
- Your sex.

A prescribed annuity offers tax deferral on non-registered funds by averaging out and deferring the interest earned over the expected life on the annuity. A prescribed annuity will have a level amount of taxable interest on an annual basis to report over the length of the contract. This ensures that the interest payments are spread evenly over the life of the annuity. Prescribed annuities are therefore not subject to the accrual taxation rules whereby interest is taxed as earned.

Certain criteria must be met to qualify for "prescribed" taxation. Some of the criteria that must be met are as follows:

- Non-registered funds must be used to purchase the annuity.
- Annuity payments must be level.
- The owner of the annuity and the individual entitled to the payments must be the same person.
- The owner of the annuity and the individual entitled to the payments may not be a corporation.
- Payments must begin in the current or next calendar year.
- Payments must not be guaranteed beyond the owner's ninety-first birthday.

Although the prescribed annuity is the most tax-effective annuity, you can also consider other types of annuities, depending on your overall financial, investment, and estate-planning strategy.

Types of Annuities
Single Life Annuity
This basic life annuity will provide you with an income stream for as long as you live. A single life annuity ensures you will never outlive your money.

Joint and Last Survivor Annuity

The joint and last survivor annuity is payable while either spouse is alive. When one spouse dies, the surviving spouse can continue receiving the same income or elect to receive a lessened amount by a given percentage. This choice is made when the annuity is purchased.

Guaranteed Term Annuity

Annuity payments can be guaranteed for a specific term, typically ranging from three to thirty years. When a guaranteed term annuity is purchased on its own, it is simply classified as a term certain annuity. However, sometimes this type of feature can be included in a single life or joint last survivor annuity, whereby upon death, guaranteed payments to named beneficiaries will continue until the term expires.

Annuities provide many benefits, and you should consider them if you are concerned about outliving your savings. Annuities should also be considered if you:

- Want to minimize tax on investment income;
- Require a secure and stable source of income;
- Do not need access to your capital;
- Are looking for diversification in your investments;
- Do not want to actively manage your investments; and
- Are looking to reduce risk and add stability to your overall investment strategy.

The following example is for a male with a 46.41% marginal tax rate and a single life annuity with a minimum guaranteed paid period of twenty years:

Comparison of Tax Payable on a Prescribed Annuity and a Non-Prescribed Annuity

Capital invested – non-registered	$200,000
Single life – guaranteed twenty-year pay	20 years
Amount of gross annuity before tax	$11,233.22
Estimated marginal tax rate	46.41%

Year	Annual taxable interest (non-prescribed annuity)	Annual taxable interest (prescribed annuity)	Cumulative net benefit of prescribed annuity
0	$0.00	$4,706.43	- $4,707.43
1	$197.39	$4,706.43	- $4,509.04
2	$8,986.26	$4,706.43	$4,279.83
3	$8,880.43	$4,706.43	$4,174.00
4	$8,770.16	$4,706.43	$4,063.73
5	$8,655.32	$4,706.43	$3,948.89
6	$8,539.04	$4,706.43	$3,832.61
7	$8,418.36	$4,706.43	$3,711.93
8	$8,293.27	$4,706.43	$3,586.84
9	$8,163.81	$4,706.43	$3,457.38
10	$8,030.15	$4,706.43	$3,323.72
11	$7,892.51	$4,706.43	$3,186.08
12	$7,751.20	$4,706.43	$3,044.77
13	$7,606.68	$4,706.43	$2,900.25
14	$7,459.49	$4,706.43	$2,753.06
15	$7,310.28	$4,706.43	$2,603.85
16	$7,160.45	$4,706.43	$2,454.02
17	$7,011.63	$4,706.43	$2,305.20
18	$6,865.56	$4,706.43	$2,159.13
19	$6,724.37	$4,706.43	$2,017.95
Total Interest Paid	$142,716.36	$94,128.60	Tax Savings $48,587.76

- Assumes that the individual's tax rate remains the same for the duration of payments.
- Single premium of $200,000 was paid on August 9, 2007.
- Annuity payment is made yearly and is guaranteed until September 9, 2026.
- Annuity payment is payable thereafter for as long as the prime annuitant is alive.

Note: The data is provided for information purposes only. Annuities are available for both registered funds and non-registered funds. Prescribed annuities are only available for non-registered funds.

Chapter 13

RESPs
(Registered Education Savings Plans)

Registered Education Savings Plans (RESPs) have two very attractive benefits. The first benefit is the tax efficiency of the plan. Although RESP contributions are not taxable, they are sheltered from taxation once the funds are invested in the plan—similar to RRSPs. The second benefit is why RESPs have been ever so popular: The Canada Education Savings Grant (CESG) matches every dollar of funds invested into a RESP with $0.20 cents up to an amount of $500 per year.

Features of RESPs:
- No maximum yearly contribution.
- Lifetime limit on RESP contributions is $50,000.
- Maximum $500 CESG payment per year unless CESG room exists from previous year, in which case the maximum CESG payment is $1,000.
- Total lifetime CESG funds payable is a maximum of $7,200.

Added benefits exist for low- and middle-income families. If a family's income is less than $37,178, for the first $500 contributed to an RESP, the combined benefits increase from 20% to 40%. This represents an additional $100 in government benefits. For middle-income families whose income is in the range of $37,178 to $74,357, the CESG is 30% on the first $500 contributed.

In Quebec, residents receive an additional refundable tax credit for education savings. The benefit is paid directly into the RESP and equates to 10% on the first $2,000 of yearly contributions for children up to eighteen years of age to a maximum amount of $3,600 over the lifetime of the plan.

Some families have sufficient wealth to fund to the maximum RESP amount in one single year. This strategy can sometimes be beneficial; however, in most cases it will not be because it would mean receiving only one to two years of CESG monies, depending on when the child was born. You should consider some factors before making large lump-sum contributions into RESPs. These factors include:

- The age of the child, as this plays a part in how long the funds will remain in the RESP;
- The type of investment returns generated, as interest, dividends, and capital gains are taxed differently outside of sheltered plans; and
- The anticipated rates of return.

Conservative investors, who would typically invest in low-yielding GICs and bonds, would probably be better off investing the lump sum in the RESP and forgoing the CESG in future years if they are in a high marginal tax bracket. Investors in high marginal tax brackets who would invest in products with high potential returns that would generate potential capital gain benefits would probably be better off moving funds annually into the RESP and receiving the added benefits of the CESG annually.

Although the contributions are not tax deductible, the savings do grow tax-free while they remain in the sheltered plan until the child is ready to attend a post-secondary school, which includes college, university, and some other educational institutions.

An RESP is specifically designed for saving for the post-secondary education of a child or other beneficiary. An RESP can be opened for a beneficiary by a parent, grandparent, family member, and even friend.

You can withdraw funds from an RESP at any time with no tax implications on principal contributions. If the withdrawal is not for post-secondary education, the withdrawal will be classified as a "capital withdrawal." Any grants, including the CESG, additional CESG grants, and the Canada Learning Bond (CLB), received on the withdrawn amount would be returned to the government at the time of withdrawal.

For withdrawals for post-secondary education, all accumulated earnings on all contributions and grants are referred to as Educational Assistance Payments (EAPs) and are taxed as income in the hands of the student. Generally, these students will have little or no income and therefore pay no or very little tax.

If the beneficiaries do not pursue post-secondary education, subscribers have many options, including:

• Selecting an alternative beneficiary, if permitted by the plan;
• Withdrawing all the contributions into the plan tax-free (grants have to be repaid);
• Withdrawing the earnings in the plan, which will be subject to tax and an additional 20% penalty*;
• Transferring up to $50,000 of the earnings in the RESP into the subscriber's RRSP or spousal RRSP assuming there is contribution room*; and
• Donating the plan's earnings to a qualifying educational institution

*The RESP must have existed for at least ten years, the contributor/subscriber must be a Canadian citizen, and all of the beneficiaries must be twenty-one years of age or older and not pursuing post-secondary education.

RESPs are available through most financial planners, banks, brokerage companies, and insurance companies. Individual self-directed RESPs are extremely flexible and can offer individuals a wide variety of products including GICs, mutual funds, stocks, and other types of investments. Pooled RESP plans are also available through organizations such as Canadian Scholarship Trusts, Global Educational Plans, Heritage Education Plans, and a few other organizations. The plans are typically geared towards individuals who are more risk adverse, as the plans have investment limitations on them and generally invest in fixed-income vehicles only. The self-directed plans provide greater flexibility in terms of investment selection.

Chapter 14
"In Trust For" (ITF) Accounts

A formal trust is created with a lawyer. In essence, it is a legal document known as a deed of trust. Although there are advantages to formal trusts, including ensuring attribution rules are managed and that the individual setting up the trust can specify the rules surrounding the assets within the trust and the age consideration of the beneficiaries, the reality is that many individuals are adequately serviced by informal trusts. Formal trusts can cost in the range of $750 to $2,500 to set up in addition to ongoing administration costs.

An informal trust is an account set up on behalf of a child by a parent, legal guardian, grandparent, aunt, uncle, or even a friend. Most financial institutions, including mutual fund companies, investment dealers, banks, and credit unions, will set up informal in-trust accounts for named beneficiaries. Income attribution rules do apply, which means that dividends and interest from the initial investment are taxed to the contributor in the year they are earned. However, capital gains and second-generation income are taxed to the beneficiary in the year they are earned.

Informal trust accounts are different from Registered Education Savings Plans (RESPs). Individuals can benefit from both RESPs and informal trusts at the same time. Informal trusts have no restrictions on how much you can invest. In addition, there is no penalty should the child or grandchild not pursue post-secondary studies. The funds automatically become the property of the beneficiary at the age of majority, which is either eighteen or nineteen years of age depending on the province the child lives in. In addition, the beneficiary can use the funds for any purpose they choose.

There is no limit in terms of contributions to the plan, as these plans are not registered as RESPs and do not qualify for the Canada Education Savings Grant (CESG). Contributions into the plan are considered gifts and held in trust for the named beneficiary. The in-trust account is a simple way of making a lump-sum contribution and letting the investment grow over time with minimal taxes paid if structured properly. Individuals can choose a variety of investments in these accounts, including GICs, bonds, mutual funds, and stocks.

Remember, however, that you should use these accounts to minimize your tax liability. Consider investments that will provide capital gains potential. If you are concerned about the safety and security of your investments, choose investments that provide principal protection along with the possibility of providing capital gains. Principal Protected Notes (PPNs) are available from over a dozen different financial institutions with principal guarantees at maturity provided by some of the largest financial institutions in Canada, the U.S., and Europe.

In terms of winding down the plan, the contributions are gifts in trust and belong to the beneficiary. The one who set up the in-trust account can withdraw the contributions and earnings if it is for the benefit of the child. Once the child reaches the age of majority, they can terminate the plan at any time.

Although the child can use the funds for any reason they choose, including vacations, fancy cars, clothing, or any other reason many would consider irresponsible, they can use them for better long-term reasons, including education, starting a business, getting married, buying a car, or buying a home.

Note that in-trust accounts are currently not available in Quebec.

Chapter 15

F-Class Funds and Management Fees

Individuals cannot deduct fees associated with the commissions charged for buying and selling securities such as stocks and mutual funds. In addition, management expense ratios (MERs) on mutual fund holdings, whether in registered plans or non-registered plans, are a non-deductible expense.

Although many Canadians own mutual funds in Canada, only a small percentage take advantage of the benefits of F-class mutual funds for non-registered investments.

F-class mutual funds are offered by fee-based financial advisors. The trailer fees of these types of investments are typically removed from the fund, and the investor can then pay a fee directly to the financial advisor for the ongoing advice. This offers two benefits in most cases:

1. Lower fees associated with holding mutual fund investments, depending on the size of the investment portfolio; and

2. The ability to deduct the associated management fees on the fee-based account, assuming the fee is for advice on whether to buy or sell securities or the management or administration of securities.

In order for the fees to be deductible, the advisor's principal role should be to advise individuals on buying and selling specific securities or to manage existing investments.

If you hold investible assets in excess of $150,000, fee-based accounts may provide you with a less expensive investment management solution as well as some potential tax deductions, provided the investment management is for non-registered investments.

The following example shows how fee-based investments and, most specifically, F-class mutual funds work. Amy is an investor who has accumulated $200,000 in non-registered funds. She is looking for advice on where to invest the funds and is considering dividend funds because they have performed well for her over the last few years.

If Amy invests the funds into TD Dividend Growth Fund, the MER on the fund is 2.09%. Instead, if she were able to invest with a fee-based advisor who is able to use F-class mutual funds, the associated fee on the actual mutual fund would be 0.086% on the TD Dividend Growth F-class fund. If the advisor charges a management fee for advice on the buying and selling of securities in the account, or for the management or administration of the account, this fee would typically be tax deductible. If the associated management fee were 1.00% per year, this amount would be tax deductible.

Assuming Amy was in a 40% tax bracket, she in essence would be paying a total fee (after considering her tax deductions) of 1.46%. This is calculated as 0.86% for the management fee on the mutual fund, which is not tax deductible, and a fee of 1.00% on the management of her account, which would provide her with a tax deduction resulting in a fee of 0.60% on the investment account. The total fee would therefore be 0.86% plus 0.60%, which equals 1.46%. Amy would save approximately 0.63%, resulting in savings in excess of $1,200 per annum.

Chapter 16

Charitable Donations

Donating assets or funds to charitable organizations, whether it is during your lifetime or through a will, can provide tax benefits to you or your estate. The donation credit provides tax relief to individuals who donate to registered charities in Canada. The first $200 donated is eligible for a federal tax credit of 15.5% of the donation amount. Depending on the province of residency, an additional provincial tax credit of 6% to 11% is available. On total donations of over $200, you can claim a federal tax credit of 29% and the additional provincial tax credits range between 11% and 18%. It is important to note that the donation credit reduces the amount of payable tax; it does not reduce your taxable income.

Spouses and common-law partners can combine their charitable donations, and the spouse with the higher taxable income should make the charitable deduction. You can carry forward donation deductions for a period of five years. In addition, you may claim donations up to 75% of your net income. In the year of death and the year prior, donations can be as high as 100% of your net income. Donations made after an individual's death through a will are treated as though they were made prior to the death and are therefore deducted on the individual's final return.

Since May 2, 2006, publicly traded securities and mutual funds can be gifted to charitable organizations, and no tax on the gain is payable. For example, let's say you purchased

1,000 shares of ABC on the Toronto Stock Exchange for a price of $1 per share, and the shares increased in value to $5 per share, triggering $4,000 in capital gains and $2,000 in taxes. Alternatively, you could donate the shares for $5,000 and not pay tax on the capital gain. A receipt is also provided for a donation of the fair market value of the securities or mutual funds on the date of the transfer.

Buy Low/Donate High Charitable Gifting Schemes

Thousands of Canadians have tried to take advantage of buy low/donate high charitable gifting schemes. These programs typically involve making a donation and receiving a receipt for a higher value than the actual cost of the donated property, which are typically products such as pharmaceuticals donated to Third World countries or things such as computer products. The Canada Revenue Agency (CRA) no longer permits these types of gifting schemes. The value of a receipt and the amount that you can claim is limited to your own cost of the property.

Chapter 17

Leveraged Investing

Borrowing to invest has become an extremely popular way to build an investment portfolio while helping reduce tax burdens. The strategy is very simple yet can be intimidating. Leverage can be done conservatively if the right structures and investments are set in place from the start. If borrowing to invest makes sense, you will be provided with a tax deduction for the interest paid on the loan. If this is the main reason for borrowing to invest, you must fully understand the tax rules.

Interest deductibility tax rules can be found in paragraph 20 (1) (c) of the Income Tax Act. In summary, the paragraph states that interest paid by a taxpayer is deductible if four conditions are met:

1. There is an obligation to pay the interest costs.
2. The interest costs must be paid or payable during the year.
3. The interest costs must be reasonable.
4. The borrowed money must be used to earn income from a business or property.

Under the Income Tax Act, income from property under the fourth condition includes interest, dividends, rents, and royalties. This means that borrowing money for investments that only provide capital gains will not be entitled to interest deductions. Ensure your advisor understands the benefits and the associated risks involved with leverage. In addition, ensure they are also knowledgeable about the Canada Revenue Agency's view on interest deductibility.

In simple terms, leverage is using other people's money to achieve your goals. Many individuals have already taken advantage of leverage. If you have a mortgage, you are using leverage. If you are making car payments, you are using leverage. If you borrowed money to invest in your RRSP, you used leverage.

With leveraged investments, you take out a loan to make an investment either as a single lump-sum purchase or over time. Each month, you make loan payments. The payments can be interest only, or both interest and principal payments. The interest paid on the loan will obviously reduce the overall investment return; however, the interest costs associated with the loan in certain cases is tax deductible. This results in a reduction in the overall costs of the strategy. In addition to providing tax deductions and tax savings, the strategy provides the benefits of compounded returns.

Although many benefits exist with leveraged investment strategies, it is important to understand the risks associated with the strategy. Leverage involves a greater amount of risk over traditional investment strategies. If you invest using borrowed funds, the gain or loss experienced will be magnified relative to the performance of the investment. If the investment loses its value, you would still be obligated to pay interest on the borrowed funds. Leveraged strategies are most suitable for individuals with long-term investment horizons of ten years or more.

Leverage is not for everyone. Ask yourself these questions when considering a leveraged strategy:
- How stable is my income?
- What is my risk tolerance?
- What is my investment time horizon?
- How much other debt do I have?

Stable income makes it easier to fund the required interest payments every month. In addition, you should consider whether you are comfortable with investments that will be volatile over time and may not outperform a regular investment strategy. You should also consider your current debt levels. Your total debt service ratio should not exceed 35% of your pretax income. This means that your total borrowing costs per month, including the costs of the investment loan, should not exceed 35% of your pretax income.

Below are the various keys to successful leverage strategies that will reduce the overall risk of the plan:

- You should invest for the long term and commit to the strategy.
- You should ignore short-term market fluctuations.
- Diversify the overall investments—diversification itself reduces risk in most situations.
- Borrow less than you can afford, especially if it's your first time in a leveraged loan strategy.
- If possible, make principal payments on your loan over time. Principal payments will reduce the magnification of potential losses. It will, however, reduce the magnification of potential gains at the same time.

Leverage is a great planning tool that can help accelerate growth and generate tax deductions over the years. Although the strategy does involve an increased level of risk, you can reduce much of it with careful planning with experienced financial planners.

Chapter 18

Making Your Mortgage Tax Deductible

Although mortgages in Canada are not directly tax deductible, there are mortgage strategies that can provide you with a creative, legal financial strategy that can generate annual tax refunds. The affluent have used some of these strategies for years. The main strategy involves converting your non-deductible interest debt, which is your mortgage interest, to tax-deductible debt.

Non-deductible interest is considered bad debt and includes loans on such things as credit cards, car loans, and especially house mortgages. Canadians in general pay a large amount of non-deductible interest every year. If this non-deductible interest were converted to deductible interest, it would generate generous tax refunds year after year.

Let's assume you have a mortgage of $100,000 at 7% per year. This would equate to approximately $6,852 in interest costs in the first year of the mortgage, which is non-deductible. If this were a tax-deductible interest expense, and if you were in a 46.4% tax bracket, you would receive a refund of approximately $3,179. If you were in a 40% tax bracket, the refund would be $2,740.

In addition to the pure tax benefits of this strategy, you will build an investment portfolio over time. With the help of experienced advisors, you can select the investments, and the purchase into these investments will begin almost immediately.

Find an advisor who is familiar with this strategy and find out whether it makes sense for you. People typically shave approximately two or three years off the amortization on a standard twenty-five-year mortgage where payments are made only on a monthly basis. If you are interested in an accelerated version of the strategy, you can shorten amortization periods by up to fifteen years in some cases. Additional information is available at www.thetaxdeductiblemortgage.com.

If you're wondering whether the strategy is legal, simply put: it is. The strategy is simple and thousands of Canadians are already using it with professional financial planners.

In addition to the tax-deductible mortgage strategy, there are other strategies to employ that can make use of your principal residence. Some individuals accumulate investment portfolios outside of registered plans greater than the size of their mortgages. If this is the case for you, it would make sense to cash in the investments and use the proceeds to pay off your mortgage. Thereafter, you can borrow funds secured by your home and invest back into new investments for your portfolio. The interest on this new secured line of credit becomes tax deductible in most cases. Discuss this strategy in depth with experienced financial advisors to ensure the selection of investments that will enable full tax deductions. For example, if your mortgage rate is 7% and you borrow the money to invest into a GIC that pays 4%, you will not be able to write off the full 7%. Asset selection is extremely important.

A word of caution for investors or those thinking of using these types of strategies without the advice and guidance of tax specialists and experienced financial planners: Be careful of the types of investments you purchase if you are buying them back. The CRA has a rule called the anti-avoidance rule that would disallow the interest deduction. To avoid this, ensure you do the following:

- Avoid investing in the same securities or investments you held prior to paying off your mortgage; and
- Obtain a new mortgage or secured line of credit secured by your bank. This will be needed to secure the loan to make the investments.

In addition, ensure any financial calculations prepared by financial planners take into consideration any capital gains liability later into the term of the strategy or during the winding down of the plan. The calculations should also be prepared using actuarial software to ensure accurate, reliable, and realistic numbers.

Chapter 19

RRSP/RRIF Meltdown Strategies

The meltdown strategy is also known as the RRSP/RRIF drawdown. The strategy helps you protect your retirement income. At the same time, it is effective in helping protect estates from full taxation when funds are withdrawn from RRSPs or RRIFs. Full taxation refers to funds withdrawn from registered plans that are added to personal income and fully taxed. In the event of death whereby a spouse is not named as a beneficiary, up to 46% could be payable in taxes. The meltdown strategy provides a variety of benefits. It has no direct impact on cash flow, and any potential tax impact of the RRSP or RRIF withdrawals are offset by the interest expense deduction on the borrowing loan.

The strategy converts income from an RRSP or RRIF into an income stream from outside of registered plans. Income that would have been taxed as regular income from being withdrawn from registered plans would be taxed at the lower capital gains rates as a result of the income being taken from non-registered funds.

To implement the RRSP/RRIF meltdown strategy, you must deal with experienced financial planners. Planners can help establish loans, since funds will be required to invest in non-registered investments that provide capital gains potential. Regular RRSP or RRIF withdrawals are then made to increase cash flow and help cover interest costs on the established loan. Ultimately, if set up efficiently, the tax on the withdrawal of funds from the RRSP or RRIF would be offset by the related interest expense on the borrowed funds. The potential benefits of the meltdown strategy should not be overlooked. The strategy has no impact on other retirement benefits, including Old Age Security. In addition, the strategy provides investment gains in non-registered accounts that would therefore be treated as capital gains and would be taxed as capital gains at a more favourable tax rate when disposed of.

You should also take estate planning into consideration. The meltdown strategy reduces the estate tax upon death. Funds are withdrawn from the RRSP or RRIF over time and the amount of funds in the registered plans therefore decreases substantially over time. By implementing the strategy, you reduce the amount of income for the beneficiaries of the estate, thereby also reducing the amount of tax paid in the final tax return in most situations.

RRSP/RRIF meltdown strategies are complex. Proper calculations must be completed to ensure the strategy is worthwhile. In most situations, the strategy may be suitable if substantial sums exist in registered plans. Since the strategy involves leverage, the plan should be considered only by those who are comfortable with the risks associated with leveraged investments and leveraged strategies. In addition, you should have a minimum of a seven- to ten-year investment horizon along with a net worth of at least two times the amount borrowed to implement the plan.

RRSP/RRIF Meltdown Strategy – Example

	RRSP Drawdown	No RRSP Drawdown	RRIF Drawdown Strategy	No RRIF Drawdown
Starting RRSP/RRIF balance	$500,000	$500,000	$500,000	$500,000
Drawdown loan	$150,000	-	$150,000	-
Loan annual interest 6%/yr	$ 9,000	-	$ 9,000	-
Minimum annual RIF withdrawal	-	-	$ 33,500	$ 33,500
Drawdown annual withdrawal	$ 9,000	-	$ 9,000	-
SUBTOTAL	$ 9,000	-	$ 42,500	-
Value of RRSP/RRIF after 10 years	$949,100	$1,079,500	$496,600	$627,000
Value of investment portfolio after 10 years	$323,800	-	$323,800	-
Net tax payable on liquidation	($414,400)	($431,800)	($233,400)	($250,800)
After-tax value of RRSP/RRIF and investment portfolio	$858,500	$647,700	$587,000	$376,200
Loan outstanding	($150,000)	-	($150,000)	-
Net after tax investments	$708,500	$647,700	$437,000	$376,200
Meltdown advantage	$60,800		$60,800	

Assumptions:

Loan rate of 6.25% per annum with interest only payments.

Cost of borrowing for full ten-year loan assumed rate of 6.25% is $90,000.

Annual rate of return on all investments assumed to be 8% per annum.

Tax rate of 40% used to calculate after-tax values.

Non-registered portfolio assumed to generate 100% capital gains only with no distributions, and therefore no tax is applicable on distributions. A 50% capital gains inclusion rate is used to calculate after-tax values.

Chapter 20

Insurance Tax Shelters
(Universal Life Insurance)

Over the last twenty years, the benefits of insurance tax shelters such as universal life (UL) insurance has become increasingly popular for those who maximize their Registered Retirement Savings Plan (RRSP) contributions and are looking for investment growth outside of registered plans. These universal life policies have become much better products than they used to be.

Life insurance companies issue these investments and they allow you to invest a sum of money and shelter the growth of the investment from income. Generally, these plans are referred to as universal life insurance plans and are available by most insurance companies and insurance advisors. Since each UL plan is unique in its own way, make sure you deal with reputable insurance advisors who can provide you with access to many reputable companies and a wider selection of products and services. Most independent insurance advisors have access to some of the larger and more reputable insurance companies such as AIG, Standard Life, Canada Life, Manulife, and many others. Ensure your advisor has access to more than just one or two insurance companies.

The CRA allows these insurance companies to issue these tax-sheltered plans as long as they maintain certain conditions. One of the conditions that must be met is that there must be a certain amount of life insurance on each plan. This type of insurance normally should be a decreasing coverage and provide only the least amount of coverage to keep the plan exempt from taxation. The amount of insurance necessary is based on a CRA formula, and each individual plan has to pass an annual test.

These plans are extremely flexible and allow you to change the amount of your deposits and choose the types of investments you are comfortable with, including GICs and index funds. UL policies are intended to be long-term investments and not a savings account. A typical investment time horizon should be at least ten to fifteen years.

When it's time to take your money out of the plan, you can do so in one of two ways. First, you can take withdrawals directly and pay no tax if the withdrawals are done in the tax-sheltered account, assuming it is not above the adjusted cost base of the plan. The adjusted cost base is equivalent to the total amount of deposits minus the actual cost of the insurance. Second, you may take further withdrawals from the plan, but they will be considered taxable by the CRA.

The main benefit of these types of plans is the leveraging available. When most people hear the word *leveraging,* they automatically think one must take equity out of their home and invest the funds into a diversified portfolio. With these types of plans, you are leveraging the actual plan and the loan is not taxable. You can therefore withdraw money from the plan and use the plan as collateral for the loan. You can withdraw a single amount of money from the plan, or you can make a series of payments that you will use as income similar to systematic withdrawal plans made available by most banks and mutual fund companies.

The insurance company will not require you to make payments on the loan since it has capitalized the loan payments. At some point, the loan is repaid from the tax-free insurance payout on death. Any excess is then paid to your beneficiaries tax-free.

If an individual dies prior to withdrawing the funds or the funds from the tax-free portion of the plan, all of the funds in the plan are then paid out to the beneficiaries tax-free. Also, because the plan is with an insurance company, it will bypass your estate and avoid probate. For those concerned about creditor-proofing their assets, investments held with insurance companies are typically creditor-proof.

Consider UL if you maximize your contributions to your RRSP and if you have no liabilities. There is no sense sheltering income in GIC-type investments in UL policies if you have existing debt, including mortgages with high rates or lines of credit either secured or unsecured. Also consider UL if you feel comfortable with equities, even if you have manageable debt.

If you are interested in seeing whether a UL policy is right for your situation, seek an advisor who is dually licensed in both the investment and insurance industries. If you deal with an individual who is only life-insurance licensed, there is a bigger incentive for them to focus on all the benefits surrounding UL policies. By engaging in relationships with reputable investment and insurance advisors, who should be able to provide you with references, you are more likely to be exposed to more products and services, which may include UL and can include other products or services mentioned in this book.

Chapter 21

Universal Life Loan Plans
(10-8 Policy Loan Programs)

Universal life (UL) loan plans may be suitable for high net worth individuals or business owners with a need for permanent insurance and those who are also interested in accumulating funds on a non-registered tax-sheltered basis.

The plans are structured to provide:
- Reduced expenses for permanent insurance protection;
- Access to funds in the policy immediately for investment capital;
- A charge set at 10% on the borrowed funds;
- Guaranteed tax deferred 8% rate of return on the loan balance; and
- A tax deduction on the annual loan interest payment.

The typical structure of a UL loan plan (10-8 program) includes the following points:
- A universal life (UL) policy is issued to the client. The policyholder could be either an individual or a holding company.
- The policyholder pays the cost of the insurance premiums on the UL policy.
- Additional deposits are made into the plan; the amounts are typically significant and can vary over time. (A maximum amount exists, as the policy wants to maintain its

tax-exempt status for income tax purposes.)
- The above-mentioned deposits are made into investment accounts under the UL plan.
- The policyholder then receives a loan from the insurance company and may receive loans in the future as well, depending on the contract and structure setup. Depending on the terms in the policy, the loans made will be up to 95% of the policy's cash surrender value.
- The policyholder will cover the 10% interest charge annually and is not required to repay the principal prior to death.
- Proceeds of the loan are invested by the policyholder in investments such as mutual funds, stocks, bonds, guaranteed investment funds, and other types of investments, including real estate and businesses.
- A transfer is made of an amount equal to the loan into an investment account under the UL policy. The account is normally called a collateral loan account and it offers the policyholder a guaranteed rate of return of 8% per year.
- Policy loan is repaid out of the insurance proceeds upon death.

The advantage of a policy loan program is that it provides individuals and business owners with a tax-deductible expense through the interest payments under the policy loan. If you are considering the benefits of a policy loan program, you should be sure to receive advice from tax experts and experienced life insurance advisors.

Individuals in a 46% tax bracket will incur an interest expense of 10%, which is fully deductible, resulting in an after-tax rate of 5.4%. The investment in the policy loan earns a guaranteed rate of return of 8% per annum and is tax sheltered, and the policyholder may receive insurance protection that is less expensive and provides more coverage than if it had been purchased as regular term or whole life insurance.

It is important to note that interest deductibility has been the subject of many disputes between the CRA and taxpayers. Borrowed funds must be used for eligible purposes and investments, and it is extremely important that you discuss strategies that involve any kind of interest deductibility with experienced financial planners and, most important, income tax advisors.

Other features and factors to consider with UL policy programs:
- Issued typically up to age eighty.
- Minimum face value of policy is $50,000.
- Minimum premiums are approximately $25,000 per year for three years.
- Available under single-life coverage and multi-life policies.

Chapter 22

Incorporating Your Business or Professional Practice

The rules and benefits for incorporation range from province to province as well as from profession to profession. Some professions allow their members to incorporate in certain provinces and some do not. For example, professions such as law, engineering, and accounting allow their members to incorporate their businesses. In Ontario, dentists can incorporate their practices, but in some other provinces, they cannot.

When professions incorporate, they are known as professional corporations (PCs). Although PCs are similar to regular corporations, they also have to follow rules set out by the organization regulating their profession.

Preferential tax rates exist for PCs on active business income earned annually up to $400,000 per year. This figure was increased from $300,000 in 2007. This limit is known as the small-business limit.

In addition to preferential tax rates, there are numerous other benefits:

- Income-splitting opportunities amongst family members.
- The accumulation of retained earnings.
- Tax deferral on corporate retained earnings.
- The ability to implement strategies including Individual Pension Plans (IPPs) and Retirement Compensation Arrangements (RCAs).
- The reduction of probate fees in some provinces.

Preferential tax rates for Canadian-controlled private corporations (CCPCs) up to the small business limit can be one of the most important factors when considering whether to incorporate your business or professional practice. The first $400,000 of active business income is taxed at a combined federal and provincial rate ranging between 16% and 22% depending on the province. Active business income does not include investment income; manufacturing and processing income; income of most financial institutions, including credit unions; deposit insurance companies; mutual fund corporations; investment corporations; and mortgage investment corporations. For example, investment income in a corporation in Ontario is taxed at a combined federal and provincial rate in excess of 49%.

Income-splitting opportunities amongst family members are possible with small business corporations and certain professional incorporations. Family members, including spouses and children (and, in some cases, parents) of the professional, are able to receive some of the corporation's after-tax income by receiving dividends on their shares of the corporation. This is possible even if the family members are not active in the corporation or professional practice. This allows family members who are potentially in lower tax brackets to receive income from dividends to ultimately lower tax liability. This might be a better strategy compared to having a single shareholder or the professional earning all the income.

The ability to accumulate retained earnings and the benefits of tax deferral should not be overlooked. It is important to note that there is no benefit if income is paid to a corporation rather than personally if all the income is paid out to the individual.

For example, if Angelo earns $300,000 per year and is contemplating the benefits of incorporation to reduce his tax liability, he would only benefit if he actually does not require $300,000 in income to cover his living expenses. If the

$300,000 was paid to the corporation and then to Angelo, no financial benefit would exist. In reality, he would probably be worse off, as the costs involved in establishing corporations and corporation tax filings are not minimal.

However, if Angelo earns $300,000 per year and only requires $100,000 of it for income and can leave the rest in the corporation, this would provide immediate tax savings, and he would see the benefits of tax deferral as well. Taxation on the corporate income would be about 20% on average and the remaining balance would be classified as retained earnings.

The bottom line is that very little benefit exists for individuals who are looking to incorporate if all of the income will be required for living expenses. To justify incorporation, an individual or professional should be able to leave a minimum of $40,000 to $50,000 in the corporation each year.

Incorporated businesses can also provide the benefits of Individual Pension Plans (IPPs) and Retirement Compensation Arrangements (RCAs), which will be discussed in chapters 23 and 24, which deal with IPPs and RCAs respectively. The contributions to the IPP and RCA would be considered a business expense and therefore be deductible against business income.

In addition to the benefits mentioned above, the $500,000 lifetime capital gains exemption for qualified small business corporations is available. This lifetime capital gains exemption is expected to increase to $750,000 as proposed in the last federal budget from April 19, 2007.

Chapter 23

Individual Pension Plans

An Individual Pension Plan (IPP) is an alternative to an RRSP that allows business owners and executives to defer taxation in far greater amounts than with an RRSP.

Currently, there are over 8,500 IPPs in Canada. A large proportion of the 1.1 million businesses in Canada employ fewer than five people. Many of them are baby boomers now in their fifties and sixties, and they are getting close to retirement. They have invested in RRSPs but do not know that they can get much larger tax deductions and build significantly larger retirement assets with IPPs.

An RRSP allows a taxpayer to save 18% of the previous year's earned income, up to a maximum dollar limit (currently $19,000 in 2007), regardless of their age. By contrast, the IPP contribution is age-related. It grows each and every year. For example, for a forty-year-old earning $110,000, the 2007 contribution is $20,800. For a fifty-year-old, the 2007 contribution is $25,000, and for a sixty-five-year-old, it is $33,600.

Why do IPP contributions grow with age? IPPs require the services of an actuary to certify the annual contributions. Actuaries calculate the value of the pension based on methods and assumptions specified in the Income Tax Act (ITA). The end result is that it produces required contributions that increase each year until retirement.

But there is more. You can also get a pension in respect

of years of past service with the company. This creates a large cost that requires supplementary tax-deductible contributions that you can fund in one installment or over a period of up to fifteen years. For example, a fifty-year-old who has earned about $100,000 or more since 1991 would be able to contribute $112,000 to fund the past service pension between 1991 and 2006.

In addition, if there is cash available in the company at the time of retirement, the ITA allows for "terminal funding" to improve the pension. This creates a tax deduction that can be in excess of $250,000.

Many actuaries offer complete solutions for a very reasonable price, so fees to set up all the documents, filings, ongoing administration, and actuary's certification make good economic sense and do not create any compliance burden on the company.

The IPP is an approach that lets you receive much larger tax deductions than you would with an RRSP. But the real benefit is that these higher contributions allow you to defer taxation on the investment growth, and this will amount to hundreds of thousands of dollars over the long term.

IPP in a Nutshell

An IPP is a "defined benefit" pension plan that provides a lifetime pension based on service and earnings with the company. The IPP must be registered with the Canada Revenue Agency (CRA) and, in most cases, with the province where you are employed. It is designed to provide the highest permissible benefits allowed under the ITA. The person participating in the IPP must be employed by a corporation and receive T4 earnings.

The objective of the IPP is to pay a lifetime pension at retirement. It is not a savings plan, but IPP owners and beneficiaries will get every last dollar in the account.

The company pays contributions in a creditor-proof trust,

making the assets separate from the corporation. Contributions are deductible to the employer and not taxable to the employee.

Permitted investments are similar to those allowed within an RRSP, except that you may not invest more than 10% of the book value in any one individual security. Plan expenses and professional fees are deductible to the company. It is also possible to deduct investment management fees if invoiced separately. Interest on loans used for paying contributions is deductible, allowing for flexibility for managing cash flow while continuing company contributions when profits or cash are low.

How It Works

Remember that an IPP is a defined-benefit pension plan. These are the pension and other benefits that are payable from an IPP:

- Pension formula: 2% x *service at retirement* x *best three-year average earnings up to the maximum allowable earnings* (currently $111,111 in 2007; this amount increases each year in line with the "average wage," a value compiled by Statistics Canada).
- The pension is payable as early as age fifty-five for life, reduced to reflect the longer expected payout for the early commencement of the pension; unreduced pension at age sixty-five.
- The pension has cost-of-living adjustments each year equal to the consumer price index minus 1%.
- Survivor pension of 66.6% of initial amount, guaranteed payable for the first five years; plan member can select the option to pay 100% survivor pension, subject to a reduction in the initial amount.
- A lump sum equal to the value of the accrued pension is payable on death before retirement or on termination of employment. Additionally, the IPP participant or the ben-

eficiaries own any surplus, so essentially all assets are paid out.

Past Service Pension and RRSP Transfer

Since 1991, the ITA has been changed to create a fair system for all taxpayers, regardless of whether they save for retirement using an RRSP or participate in a defined-benefit plan. RRSP contributions are 18% of the previous year's earned income, up to a maximum dollar limit, less a pension adjustment (PA). The pension adjustment reflects the value of the company pension that accrues during the year.

If someone is in a company pension plan, the maximum RRSP contribution is reduced and the taxpayer does not receive larger tax-deferral opportunities than someone who has no company pension plan. In other words, the pension adjustment is a way to eliminate "double dipping"—that is, getting full RRSP contributions and a pension from a company plan at the same time.

If we take our example of a fifty-year-old business owner, the IPP contribution for 2007 is $25,000. This will generate a PA of $19,400. Therefore, the allowable RRSP contribution for 2008 will be $20,000 less $19,400—or $600.

Providing past service in the IPP gives rise to a "past service pension adjustment" (PSPA). The PSPA reduces the maximum RRSP contribution room in the years that make up the past service pension.

If the IPP were set up in 1991, there would have been a PA for each year and RRSP contributions would have been reduced as described above. The PSPA is a one-time adjustment to the RRSP room that reflects the accrual of a company pension benefit for each of these years.

If there is an existing RRSP deduction limit, the PSPA will usually eliminate it. The remaining amount for the PSPA will be approved by doing a "qualifying transfer" between the RRSP and IPP.

In our example, assuming our business owner has made full RRSP contributions since 1991, there would be a transfer of $273,000 from the RRSP to the IPP in order for the CRA to approve the past-service pension. They will approve it if there are sufficient RRSP assets, an existing RRSP deduction limit, or combination thereof. If they cannot approve it, then the past-service pension is reduced to the amount that will be approved.

The value of the past-service pension calculated by the actuary in our example is $385,000. The IPP gets an amount of $273,000 by way of a transfer of RRSP assets, so there is a funding shortfall of $112,000. This amount can be funded in one installment or over a period not exceeding fifteen years.

Options at Retirement

There are three options available for dealing with accumulated funds at retirement.

The first approach is you can maintain the IPP and pay the pension from the trust fund. This requires ongoing administration and actuarial valuations every three years. If you live very long, say above age ninety, the IPP may run out of money. The company that sponsors the plan can make up the shortfall either by injecting more (tax-deductible) money or winding up the plan.

The second approach is to buy an annuity from an insurance company. This can be a costly option, as annuity premiums can be quite high in a low-interest environment. If the IPP participant and spouse are deceased after a few years, there would be no further assets available to the estate or beneficiaries. Conversely, if you live to age 120, the pensions will continue to be paid and the plan will never run out of money.

The third approach is to transfer the funds to a locked-in retirement account before age seventy-one, or a life income fund after that age. This last option sometimes results in a portion of the funds being deemed "taxable excess in cash." For example, if the IPP has an accrued pension of $90,000 at age sixty-two and $1,400,000 in assets, only $1,080,000 would be allowed to be transferred directly into the locked-in account. The difference of $320,000 would be paid in cash and subject to personal income tax. This tax bill can be mitigated by arranging to receive it in a year with reduced income, deferring withdrawals from the locked-in assets for a later year. In addition, transferring from the IPP creates a "pension adjustment reversal" (PAR), and this creates significant RRSP room that may allow for a RRSP deduction that may offset some of this negative effect.

Additionally, assets are locked-in, which means you cannot cash them out in a single (taxable) lump sum. However, some jurisdictions do not require locking-in for IPP-transferred assets (e.g. British Columbia and Quebec) or allow a portion to be unlocked (25% in New Brunswick and Ontario after 2007, 50% in Manitoba). Life income funds are quite flexible and almost no jurisdictions require the purchase of an annuity after age eighty. Permitted annual withdrawals are any amount between the minimum withdrawal required for a Registered Retirement Income Fund (RRIF) and a maximum withdrawal based on age-related percentages that vary from province to province. The maximum withdrawal percentages increase each year and typically reach 100% when the person reaches age ninety. It is possible in most jurisdictions to unlock the assets and cash them out if the person has a "reduced" life expectancy or if the account balance is very small. This means the whole account can be cashed out eventually. Choosing which approach is best depends on individual circumstances. In any case, this decision can be made at the time of retirement.

Terminal Funding

As mentioned above, it is possible to improve certain benefits at the time of retirement and contribute a significant amount in a lump sum to fund the improvements. This optional funding is called "terminal funding." Improvements to benefits consist of providing an unreduced early retirement pension at age sixty or a slightly reduced pension between fifty-five and sixty, a supplementary temporary pension equal to the CPP pension until age sixty-five, and cost-of-living adjustments in line with the full increase in the consumer price index (as opposed to CPI minus 1%).

Opportunity to Make Up for Poor Investment Returns

At any time during the life of the plan, if poor investment returns or other factors create a shortfall of assets, as determined by the actuary, pension legislation requires the company to make supplementary company contributions to eliminate the shortfall over a period not exceeding five years. Compare this to an RRSP. With turbulent capital markets, low or negative returns are a definite possibility, but there is no opportunity to put more money in the RRSP above the maximum contributions. With an IPP, if the assets are not on track for paying the pension at retirement, the actuary will calculate supplementary contributions that are tax deductible to the company. This is a great way to manage investment risk while getting a tax break at the same time.

New Approach: Deducting Investment Management Fees

A new trend in the last few years has been to arrange for the investment manager to separately invoice investment management fees (IMFs) and have them paid by the company as a deductible business expense.

For example, if there is $300,000 in the IPP and IMFs are 2% of assets per year, this means the company gets a $6,000 deduction for the year. This deduction is available each year and increases in line with the growing assets. Best of all, it does not create a taxable benefit to the IPP participant.

Another complementary approach is to allow the plan to have "additional voluntary contributions" (AVCs). The IPP participant can elect to have AVCs and transfer the full balance of their RRSP in the IPP.

If, for example, the remaining RRSP assets are $400,000, with a 2% IMF, this creates a deduction for the company of another $8,000. Deducting IMFs are not allowed for an RRSP, only for AVCs, held in a registered pension plan.

Although assets are commingled in the account, a sub-account is kept for the AVCs and they retain a status similar to RRSP assets with no locking-in provisions.

IPP contributions are already higher than that of RRSPs, so this strategy makes it possible to make larger deposits in the IPP that will enjoy tax-deferred growth, and this creates an advantage that can over time almost double the effectiveness of the IPP.

Implementing the IPP

Your investment advisor can recommend an actuarial firm that will prepare all the documents. These consist of a board of directors' resolution, a legal pension plan document, a trust agreement (if plan is self-trusteed), an actuarial valuation report, a statement of investment policies and procedures, and an application and other forms from the CRA and the provincial pension supervisory authority.

Annual compliance includes the preparation of a trust return, an annual information return, filing of unaudited account statements, an investment income summary, and Form 7 – Statement of Contributions (Ontario). Ongoing actuarial valuations are required every three years.

The actuarial firm should be able to do all this for a reasonable fee. Also, the firm should have "specimen" documents pre-approved with the CRA. This ensures fast-track registration and much lower implementation costs.

To implement the IPP, you must supply the actuary with T4 earnings for each year of past service, the amount of the RRSP deduction limit for the previous year, and the market value of the RRSP at the end of the previous year.

In order to help you decide if an IPP is a good idea, the actuarial firm introduced by your financial advisor or accountant will provide you with estimated contributions for past and current service, future estimated assets, and annual pensions at no cost. This way, you can use accurate information to decide whether to go ahead. All you have to do is arrange for passing a board of directors' resolution to implement the legal plan documents and sign application forms and other compliance documents. Most jurisdictions charge a small fee to register the pension plan with the provincial pension authority. For example, the fee for Ontario is $250.

You must also open a trust account. The plan can have individual trustees, at least three persons (one of whom is independent of the company), or can use a corporate trustee. Your investment advisor and actuary will help you open the account and set up the trusts. A few corporate trustees charge very reasonable fees in the range of $300 per year. Note that even if you open the trust account, no contributions may be paid before the plan registration has been acknowledged by the CRA.

IPP Setup Checklist
❏ Plan document
❏ Trust agreement (standard document)
❏ Pension plan booklet (standard document)
❏ Actuarial valuation
❏ Board of directors' resolution
❏ Statement of investment policies and procedures (standard document)

❏ Registration, application, and other forms for provincial authority and CRA

❏ Qualifying transfer (amount going from RRSP to IPP) and past-service pension adjustment (reduces RRSP room)

IPP Annual Compliance Checklist

❏ Trust return

❏ Annual information return

❏ Investment statement filing

❏ Investment income summary, Form 7 – Statement of Contributions (Ontario)

❏ Pension adjustment amount on T4

❏ Annual pension statement to IPP participant

❏ Actuarial valuation (every third year)

Ideal Candidates for an IPP

Any owner/manager of small- or medium-sized business; highly-paid executive; owner of a franchise; a professional who is able to incorporate, such as an accountant, dentist, engineer, lawyer, physician, or business executive, can greatly benefit by setting up an IPP.

Here is a profile of an ideal candidate for an IPP:

• An owner of a small- or medium-sized incorporated business.

• Has been incorporated for several years to maximize past-service deductible contributions.

• Aged forty to fifty-five, with earnings at $100,000 or above, and with good cash flow in the company.

• Aged fifty-five to sixty-five and wants to take cash out of the company in a tax-effective manner.

• Has a need to create retirement wealth that is separate from the company's assets.

- Has a need to have creditor-proof assets.
- Will approach and retain a non-shareholder executive by providing tax-effective compensation.

Advantages of an IPP
- Reduction of current income tax payable by the corporation.
- Alternative to taxable bonus income or after-tax retained earnings for business owners.
- Deferral of income tax until retirement, when tax rates will be lower.
- Maximization of tax-deferred investment growth.
- Increase in net worth through higher and ongoing annual contributions.
- Creation of an inflation-indexed lifetime income that is an important component of retirement security.
- Creditor-proof assets held in a trust, separate from the company's assets.

Disadvantages, or Perceptions vs. Reality
Age. An IPP is not appropriate for someone younger than forty. It is better to maximize RRSPs until about age forty, and then switch to the IPP at that time. The reason is because the IPP contributions are age-related, and during your twenties and thirties, the contributions will be below what is allowed in an RRSP.

Fees. Fees will be higher than maintaining a self-directed RRSP. Depending on the firm and the level of service provided, the actuary's fees will range from $1,500 to $5,000. It is best to shop around and find a vendor that has a reasonable cost structure. Note that all fees are a valid deductible business expense.

Complexity. The arrangement is far more complex than an RRSP. With an RRSP, you make contributions, invest the money, and make withdrawals during retirement. The complexity lies in determining how much money you will need to maintain your lifestyle and how much you can withdraw each year without outliving your assets.

An IPP will pay the annual pension based on the service and earnings at retirement. The actuary will make sure you have enough money to pay the pension, so the risk of outliving assets because of excessive withdrawals is greatly reduced.

A way to look at this is by considering that complexity is the trade-off for going after the much larger tax-deferral opportunity provided by an IPP. However, a good actuarial firm will handle all the compliance and administration seamlessly for a reasonable fee, and the investment advisor will deal with the assets, so the business owner requires a very small time investment dealing with the plan.

Terms of Payment

The pension payable at retirement will be based on service and earnings at retirement. For example, if the IPP participant retires in ten years with maximum allowable earnings of $150,000 and twenty-five years of service, the pension payable in the first year of retirement will be $75,000. It will increase each year in line with inflation.

There is no way to draw $200,000 for ten years or alter the annual income once it starts. However, it is possible to transfer the funds into a life income fund (see *Options at Retirement* above) and achieve greater flexibility with the terms of payment. Although these funds will be locked-in, changes to locking-in rules in many provinces now allow for a one-time unlocking of a significant portion of assets (e.g. 25% in Ontario, effective January 1, 2008). These payments are taxable as income, so personal tax rates apply, unlike dividends or capital gains, which enjoy a more preferential tax treatment.

For many business owners, an IPP will be one part of the retirement income solution. In addition to this, an affluent person will receive the CPP retirement pension and will likely have significant non-registered assets and an RRSP, so the total annual income will be sufficient to maintain their lifestyle throughout retirement.

IPP "Top 10" Objections

Objection 1: Contributions are inflexible, what if I can't afford it?
A few options are available to deal with this situation:
* Amend the plan to reduce or cancel future accruals (and get them back later when you can afford it).
* Wind-up the plan.
* If you pay yourself less, then the contributions will be lower since they are based on a percentage of your pay. This will affect the ultimate pension payout.
* Use the company line of credit or get a corporate loan; the interest on the loan is deductible to the business.

Objection 2: I won't be able to contribute to a spousal RRSP. This is a misconception:
* If your spouse is on payroll, in addition to implementing an income-splitting strategy before retirement, they can be in the IPP for larger IPP deductible contributions.
* Spousal RRSPs have lost most of their appeal following the 2007 budget, which now allows a couple to split pension income.
* IPP pension income is an eligible type of income that can be split between spouses.

Objection 3: IPPs are too complex and too costly.
We touched on this before, but it can be summarized as follows:

- Benefits of tax deductions and tax-deferred growth far outweigh complexity and fees.
- Be your own trustee (it's free), or use a low-cost trust company.
- Sometimes a business owner's accountant may have limited familiarity with these arrangements and will label them as too complex. The thing to remember is that they are not in charge of your retirement security, you are. Their expertise is helping you solve business issues, not personal finance issues. But as a business owner, you can merge both with an IPP: increase company deductions and create retirement security.

Objection 4: Too much administration and paperwork.
- Outsourcing makes administration seamless.

Objection 5: I don't want to have my assets locked-in.
- For an affluent person, this will not be the only asset.
- If retirement is around the corner, annual income is available.
- Money becomes unlocked if life expectancy is shortened. Some jurisdictions allow 25% or 50% of the assets to be unlocked, and this should provide enough flexibility.

Objection 6: I don't have enough RRSPs to buy back past service.
- You can use up your RRSP room.
- If this is not enough, limit past service to what is allowed with the current RRSP balance.
- Future service contributions will still be significantly above what is allowed in an RRSP.

Objection 7: I can't contribute to an RRSP if I have an IPP.
- You can't have your cake and eat it too: RRSPs and pension plans are integrated to avoid double dipping.

- Because IPP contributions are based on the discounted value of the future pension payable, they increase with age as retirement draws closer.
- RRSP contributions are higher than IPP contributions until the late thirties, and from the forties onward, the IPPs contributions are increasingly higher than RRSP contributions until retirement.

Objection 8: The IPP will not generate enough income.
- The IPP is a piece of your retirement solution and will provide a much higher income than your RRSP, unless your RRSP has consistent spectacular returns over the long term.
- It would be imprudent to assume that the best outcome is what will happen. In any case, to achieve higher returns, you need to take higher risk, and the outcome is less certain in these volatile and uncertain times.

Objection 9: I will lose withdrawal flexibility.
- You will gain income stability.
- You will also get a guaranteed inflation-indexed income you can count on for the rest of your life.

Objection 10: There will be taxable excess if I transfer to a locked-in plan at retirement.
- Taxable excess can be mitigated by the pension adjustment reversal, which restores some RRSP room and creates the opportunity for a large tax deduction.
- View it as extra income in the first year of retirement to spend on a special expense, such as a vacation property or boat.
- If it's your intention to transfer, the plan should limit its contributions to minimize the taxable excess.

The retirement of many entrepreneurs is closely tied to the success of their businesses. Their only strategy for retirement is RRSP contributions and after-tax savings.

The IPP is a strategy that will help the business owner meet future lifestyle needs with maximum tax effectiveness. These arrangements can dodge two tax bullets at once: Company contributions are not taxable to business owners and are a tax-deductible expense to the company.

The IPP is also the answer to these key retirement planning issues:

- Inadequacy of present and future RRSP limits, with much larger IPP contributions.
- Creation of a lifetime inflation-indexed income to maintain standard of living.
- Peace of mind knowing you cannot outlive your money.
- Protection of wealth against low investment returns.
- Getting the most out of investments with tax-free growth of investment income.
- Providing a survivor income to a spouse after the business owner's death, and leaving assets to the estate.

Selecting a good actuarial firm that has streamlined the implementation process, including creating legal documents that are pre-registered with the CRA, trust agreements, investment policy statements, and valuation reports, allows the company to do a seamless and cost-effective implementation. This strategy creates large corporate deductions that you can invest on a tax-sheltered basis and are not otherwise available with any other approach. But the most important benefit is ensuring that the business owner can enjoy what they deserve for their lifetime of efforts: financial security for themselves and their family.

IPP Essentials

Below is a summary of all the features of the IPP:

- The IPP pays a pension based on earnings and service.
- The IPP is a registered pension plan of the "defined benefit" type that provides the highest permissible benefits allowed under the Income Tax Act of Canada.
- It is not a savings plan, but the IPP participant or beneficiary will get every last dollar in the account.
- The IPP participant must use any available RRSP room and/or transfer some RRSP assets at inception in exchange for getting a past-service pension (past-service pension adjustment).
- The IPP replaces the RRSP with only $600 per year allowed to go in the RRSP going forward.
- The IPP can be set up only by a corporation. The IPP participant must receive T4 income. This arrangement is not available to self-employed individuals or incorporated business owners who pay themselves a management fee or dividends.
- The company pays the contributions, not the individual. They are deductible to the company and not taxable to the employee.
- Contributions are deposited in a creditor-proof trust. IPP assets are separate from the company.
- Contributions to the IPP in respect of current service increase with age. Starting in their late thirties, they exceed what is allowed in an RRSP.
- Contributions in respect to past service are paid all at once or funded over time during a period that does not exceed fifteen years.
- Current and past-service contributions are limited by the CRA, but they are still much higher than the maximum RRSP contributions.
- The IPP pays a lifetime pension at retirement to the IPP participant and a survivor pension to the spouse. A lump

sum is payable at termination of employment or death.

- The IPP pension is 2% of indexed earnings per year of service with the company. Covered earnings are $111,111 in 2007 and increase each year in line with the average wage, a measure compiled by Statistics Canada. The pension can start as early as age fifty-five, subject to a reduction, at sixty-five with no reduction, or be deferred as late as age seventy-one.
- The survivor pension payable to the spouse is 66.6% of the amount payable to the IPP participant. It is guaranteed payable for the first five years even if both spouses become deceased during that period. The survivor pension can be increased to 100% of the amount payable to the IPP participant, subject to a reduction in the initial amount at retirement.
- The pension is increased each year in line with the change in the consumer price index (CPI) minus 1%.
- Optional funding is available at retirement (called terminal funding) to improve the following benefits:
  - Provide an unreduced early retirement from age sixty, or a pension subject to a smaller reduction before age sixty.
  - Pay a temporary "bridge" pension equal to the amount payable by the CPP, until it becomes payable at age sixty-five.
  - Fully index the pension, as opposed to providing a pension indexed at CPI minus 1%.
- If the spouse is on the company payroll, the business owner can include the spouse in the IPP (sometimes referred to as a "2PP"—that is, an IPP with two persons in it).
- Investments are similar to RRSPs, except that no more than 10% of the book value may be invested in any one individual security.
- Expenses for the setup and maintenance of the IPP are

deductible. This includes professional fees and investment management expenses.

- Poor returns that create a shortfall in the plan can be made up with extra contributions as determined by the actuary.
- The options at retirement are: paying the pension from the trust fund, buying an annuity, or transferring the assets to a locked-in retirement account or life income fund. The latter will give rise to a taxable excess amount in cash.

Bonus: Tax Deductions and Tax-Deferred Growth
If tax-deferred growth makes an RRSP a wonderful retirement savings strategy, then it makes an IPP even better. This is because the IPP's higher contributions will have a much larger amount benefiting from this tax-deferred growth.

We look at RRSPs as an attractive strategy because of the tax deductions we get each year. After all, every dollar of tax saved is a dollar invested. However, the main benefit commonly overlooked is the benefit of the tax-deferred growth in the plan.

Are more tax deductions and tax-deferred growth better? Yes, because of the magic of tax-deferred compounding. Albert Einstein called compound interest "the greatest invention of all time." This is because the growth is exponential.

Not only does capital earn interest but the interest it earns also earns interest. This creates a snowball effect over time. This phenomenon is also at play with amounts invested in capital markets and fluctuating investment returns from year to year. And this compounding wonder is magnified if you don't have to pay income tax on investments. There is simply more money on which to compound your investments.

Consider the following retirement savings scenarios. You invest in non-registered investments: You get to pay tax on your income and invest what is left over. If it is an amount of $20,000 and you are at the top marginal tax rate in Ontario, you would pay about $9,200 in income tax on the bonus and have $10,800 available to invest. You would then invest this amount and pay income tax each year on interest and dividend income, and realized capital gains.

This option can be made most attractive by following a buy-and-hold approach, and taxes would then be deferred as long as possible until capital gains are realized. This is a risky approach because it means assets must be invested in equities, unless corporate class mutual funds are purchased, which allows for maintaining a diversified portfolio without triggering capital-gains tax when rebalancing the assets.

The other scenario is investing in a savings arrangement that uses before-tax dollars and allows for tax-deferred growth, such as in an RRSP. With this approach, instead of receiving an amount of $20,000, you would instead invest it in the RRSP and get a tax refund of $9,200, using the same example as above. The full amount of capital invested would be deferred until it is paid out, at which time it would be taxed as income. But the most important benefit is that the tax-deferred growth of investment income would be much higher because no tax is payable during the deferral period. This allows more money to compound and creates a much larger value over time, all other things being equal. In addition to this, you can invest the refund in a non-registered account.

So in a nutshell, tax-deferred growth has a greater impact than tax deductions. Exponential growth is best achieved in a tax-deferred account. It is better to pay tax later rather than now. It is the best strategy because most people will have less income during retirement, meaning personal income tax rates will be lower. Deferring tax also means more money is available to transfer to the surviving spouse in a lower bracket in case of early death.

Tax Deductions and Tax-Deferred Growth Comparison
This table compares a few of the most common approaches to wealth creation that are available in Canada.

Arrangement	Annual Tax Deductions	Tax-Deferred Growth	Payout
Registered Retirement Savings Plan (RRSP)	$19,000 in 2007 Increasing to $22,000 in 2010	Yes	Taxed as income when paid, possibly at a lower rate during retirement
Individual Pension Plan (IPP) *	Annually: $19,000 – $34,000 – Past service: $50,000 – $200,000 At retirement: $100,000 – $250,000	Yes	Taxed as income when paid, possibly at a lower rate during retirement
Retirement Compensation Arrangement (RCA)	Any amount: $50,000 – $1,000,000+	No, unless investments are tax-deferred, such as corporate class mutual funds or permanent or universal life insurance	Taxed as income when paid, possibly at a lower rate during retirement; taxed at 15% to 25% if emigrating from Canada
Health & Welfare Trust	Any eligible medical expenses	N/A	Non-taxable
Registered Education Savings Plan (RESP)	No, but has government matching	Yes	Non-taxable to student child
Non-Registered Investments	No, must use after-tax dollars	Depends on nature of investment (interest, dividends or capital gains)	Non-taxable

* IPP annual contributions are age-related; this example assumes maximum eligible earnings of $111,111 in 2007 and service since 1991.

Individual Pension Plan Chart

The following chart summarizes the operation of the Individual Pension Plan.

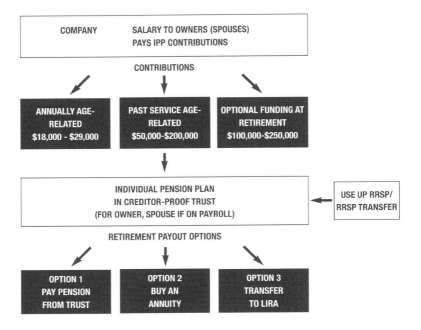

To consider whether an IPP makes sense for you, find an accredited financial planner who has adequate experience setting up and managing Individual Pension Plans. Ensure the planner has a relationship with an actuary who can provide the calculations required to determine the suitability of the strategy and help handle the set up of the plan if so desired. (Please see Appendix 2.)

Chapter 24

Retirement Compensation Arrangements (RCA)

Issues for Business Owners and Professionals

When thinking about creating wealth and financial security personally and for their families, business owners and professionals face many issues. What is the best approach to minimize high income tax? How can they maintain their standard of living during retirement after employment income ceases? How can they protect assets from creditors in case of a legal liability to the company or unforeseen bankruptcy? How can they take money from the company and not have all their wealth tied up with the fortunes of the company?

Small/medium business owners, professionals, and executives earning over $200,000 have to pay a lot of income tax and enjoy few risk-free tax deductions to help maximize their wealth and create a retirement stream of income.

For a high-income earner, an RRSP will not be large enough to fuel their lifestyle during retirement, so they must pay income tax and save and invest money in a non-registered account.

A Retirement Compensation Arrangement (RCA) is a valuable alternative to RRSPs: Contributions are tax deductible to the company and not taxable to the RCA participant, assets are in a creditor-proof trust account, and the funds saved and invested are used to provide a post-retirement stream of income to the business owner and their spouse or beneficiary. It can also be a powerful tool for business succession planning and a sale of the assets of a business.

Traditionally, business owners pay a taxable bonus at the end of the year to reduce the profit below the small-business deduction limit, pay corporate tax on the rest, and build retained earnings. Eventually, these funds may be paid as dividends, or the owner may implement a strategy to take advantage of the "special capital gains exemption" of $750,000. Paying dividends means that the overall tax paid by the corporation is about the same as if the funds were paid straight out as a bonus in the hands of the business owner.

Taking advantage of the special capital gains exemption is a good strategy if the business assets held by the corporation are sufficient to meet the eligibility tests. However, certain professions that are allowed to incorporate cannot create a holding company or apply a similar strategy, so this option is not always possible. If the special capital gains exemption is used up or is not available, then the only tax-effective retirement strategies that remain are the Individual Pension Plan (IPP) and the RCA.

RCAs may be an ideal solution for newly incorporated professionals, such as dentists and physicians. Since the maximum eligible earnings in an IPP are only about $110,000 and there is little service in the corporation from which to create a past-service pension in the plan, an RCA may be an ideal solution, as all earnings are eligible. Moreover, if a business owner has substantial earnings but low earnings during several years in the past, the IPP pension would be reduced. With the RCA, in establishing the pension, the amount is calculated based on the best average earnings, not career earnings. This makes a tremendous difference in the amount that can be tax-sheltered.

Most public companies provide RCAs for their senior executives, and a growing number of business owners and incorporated professionals use this strategy as their main source of retirement income, so there must be something good about them!

What Is an RCA?

An RCA is a type of pension plan for executives and high-income earners allowed by the Income Tax Act (ITA) of Canada.

The RCA is defined in subsection 248(1) of the ITA. An employer, former employer, or, in some cases, an employee makes contributions to a custodian. The custodian holds the funds in a trust with the intent of eventually distributing them to the employee (beneficiary) on, after, or in view of retirement; on any other severance from employment; or after any substantial change in the services the employee provides.

For a high-income earner, the tax-assisted savings of an RRSP, IPP, or registered pension plan cannot allow for the accumulation of capital necessary to provide for the family's financial needs during retirement.

A corporation can set up an RCA to fund retirement benefits that go far beyond RRSPs and registered pension plans. RCAs have been allowed under the ITA since 1986. Currently, there are about 2,500 RCAs in Canada.

There are no restrictions on how much you can put away in an RCA. The contributions are fully deductible by the company and not taxable to the employee, and the assets are held in-trust separate from the company and are creditor-proof.

How Does an RCA Work?

Under an RCA, amounts are deposited in a trust and investment proceeds are payable at termination of employment (loss of office), at retirement or death as a lifetime pension, in a lump sum, or as a series of installments. Contributions to an RCA are 100% deductible to the company and not taxable to the employee until paid out.

Unlike RRSPs, DPSPs, and defined contribution pension plans, an RCA has no limit on the amount of contributions and retirement benefits that can be paid to an employee, making them ideal for executives, business owners, and high-income earners. The only requirement is that contributions and benefits be reasonable in light of the employee's service and earnings.

Unlike IPPs, which cover only about the first $110,000 of earnings, all earnings under an RCA can be recognized in the determination of benefits. Moreover, RCAs are not covered by provincial pension legislation, which means that there are no compliance requirements and especially no locking-in of assets. The taxpayer can still contribute to their personal RRSP while participating in the RCA. Unlike IPPs, the terms of payment can be altered and pension payments are not restricted to a lifetime pension.

With an RCA, the company enters into a trust agreement with a corporate trustee or individual trustees. The employee can act as their own trustee and custodian of the funds and decide on the investments, or they can retain the services of an investment advisor. At retirement, termination of employment, or death, the company hands over the administration to the beneficiary of the trust.

Some Examples of RCAs

Business owner A is forty-two years old with twelve years of service and earns $200,000. Setting up an RCA today would allow a lump-sum contribution of $980,000 plus annual contributions of $68,000, or annual contributions of $180,000 over ten years. At age fifty-five, the deductible contributions would accumulate safely in a trust worth over $2,500,000. The owner and spouse could draw annual income of $200,000 over fifteen years.

Business owner B is fifty-seven years old with twenty-five years of service and earns $350,000. Setting up an RCA today would allow a lump-sum contribution of almost $2,000,000, which could be drawn as retirement income over several years.

Let's also consider a dentist who has just created her professional corporation, is forty years old, and earns $300,000. The RCA annual contribution will be $92,000 per year, and at age sixty-five, assets in the RCA will be $3,400,000.

When Is an RCA Appropriate?

The RCA is often appropriate where company ownership is closely held or has non-shareholder senior executives. The RCA makes it possible to obtain significant corporate tax deductions, defer amounts for payment after retirement, reduce the current tax burden of profitable companies, and is an attractive alternative to highly taxed bonus payments and dividends paid from retained earnings. It is a way to create a post-retirement stream of income that will provide adequate income to the employee, their spouse, their children, or other beneficiary, making it an effective intergenerational wealth-transfer tool.

The RCA is also a risk-free wealth-preservation tool, since the assets are held in trust separate from the company and protected from creditors.

Why Are RCAs Not That Common?

Since registered pension plans provide inadequate coverage relative to executive compensation, the primary use of RCAs has traditionally been to provide comparable security for their pension promise, in particular for public companies. RCAs can be very expensive to set up and maintain, but they can also be set up in a way that is streamlined and cost-effective.

RCAs usually require the specialized skills and professional qualifications of an actuary for the design and valuation of the arrangement. There are about 2,600 qualified actuaries in Canada, but only a few practice in this area, and even fewer provide services to small- and medium-sized businesses. (Please see Appendix 2.)

Because RCAs require the involvement of an actuary, accountants are often not familiar with them and rely on other strategies for tax minimization, such as paying out bonuses or dividends to maintain the small-business deduction exemption.

With more and more business owners inching toward retirement, business succession and financial security are now increasingly coming to the forefront. With reasonable setup costs, a streamlined implementation, outsourced administration, and self-trusteed or low-cost trust arrangements, the RCA is becoming a cost-effective strategy that deserves serious consideration.

Who Should Consider Establishing an RCA?

The following is a profile for the ideal RCA candidate:

- An incorporated business of any size.
- A professional corporation, such as dentist, physician, accountant, etc.
- A highly paid non-shareholder executive seeking security of pension promise.
- Wants to create "golden handcuffs" for non-shareholder executive.
- Is aged forty to seventy, personal income above $150,000 per year, good cash flow.
- Wants a tax shelter for the proceeds from the sale of assets of a business.
- Is concerned about business succession planning and preserving company assets between generations.

How to Setup an RCA

Setting up an RCA can be very expensive if you use multiple professionals and get a completely customized arrangement. In such a case, you would retain the services of a law firm and an actuarial consulting firm, whose fees would be significant.

Alternatively, you can select an actuarial firm or vendor that provides a standardized product at a much lower cost. Your advisor can help you find a reputable vendor with reasonable fees. These vendors will also provide a free estimate of annual contributions, future assets, and pensions, so you can see the possibilities before deciding if you want to go ahead.

A good advisor will have a team of professionals at their disposal, giving you access to high-level advice on all financial strategies and tax- and estate-planning issues. For RCAs, you should know that a qualified actuary is the only expert recognized by law for the implementation and funding of pension plans and income-security programs. Only actuaries are allowed by legislation to certify pension plan liabilities and contribution requirements of registered pension plans. For RCAs, the CRA wants to see an actuary's certificate to confirm that the RCA is a bona fide pension arrangement.

The actuarial firm or RCA provider will do everything required to set up the arrangement; do the annual compliance work; and have discussions with the client, advisor, and accountant on the timing and magnitude of desired annual contributions. It is the advisor's job to invest the tax-deductible contributions and annual cash flow.

You will have to open a trust account in the name of the RCA. This is where the contributions will be deposited and invested. The business owner can be their own trustee, or there can be a few trustees, one of whom is at arm's length from the company. The company is also responsible to make the remittance payment to the refundable tax account before the 15th of the month following the date of the contribution.

Implementing an RCA
These are the documents required to implement an RCA:
- Plan document and trust agreement

- Actuarial valuation
- Board of directors' resolution
- T733 Form (application for an RCA account number)

RCA Annual Compliance
- T3-RCA tax return
- T735 – application for a remittance number for tax withheld from an RCA
- T4A-RCA and T4A-RCA summary to report benefits paid from an RCA
- T737 RCA summary and supplementary to report company contributions
- Actuarial valuation (not less frequently than every three years)

IPP and RCA Combined?

Should a business owner have both an IPP and RCA? It depends. The IPP will be more tax-effective than the RRSP for sure, but there will be two plans with trust accounts to maintain indefinitely. In this regard, the business owner may be better off selecting either just an IPP or a combination of RRSP and RCA.

The choice of choosing between an IPP and an RCA comes down to the following considerations:

- The level of flexibility in contributions and income payments: The RCA is completely flexible; the IPP requires continued contributions unless the plan is amended or wound up.
- The desire for maximum tax-effectiveness: The IPP is better here, with tax-deferred growth of all investment income; only half of the RCA's assets can be invested, with the other half on deposit in the refundable tax account with the CRA earning no interest.
- The level of desired income: The RCA does not have any limits; the IPP caps eligible earnings at $111,000 (in 2007).

- Earnings history and length of service: If the business owner had "lean" years in the company with low income, the past service pension in the IPP will be low, as the pension is calculated in terms of "indexed" earnings as opposed to highest average earnings for the RCA.
- The level of current income: For non-shareholder executives, the IPP may be the best approach for employees earning between $100,000 and $200,000, while the RCA would be best for those earning between $200,000 to above $1,000,000 per year.

RCA with Universal Life and RCA Loans

While the investments that you may use to fund an RCA are completely flexible, a large share of them were funded with permanent or universal insurance. This is because it allows for the deferral of investment income in the RCA trust account. Otherwise, 50% of any realized investment income (interest, dividends, and realized capital gains) in the trust account has to be deposited each year in the refundable tax account, which bears no interest. And since there is a death benefit, this approach may be justified only if there is an insurance need to be met. Corporate class mutual funds can achieve deferral of investment income just as well without the fees associated with the insurance policy and the cost of insurance. In addition, universal policies require continued contributions to maintain their tax-exempt status, which defeats the contribution flexibility that is one of the big advantages of an RCA.

Many business owners have been attracted to the idea of borrowing back as much as 90% of the assets held in the insurance policy and refundable tax account as a source of capital for the business. This is an expensive and controversial strategy and the CRA has publicly commented many times that if they see the RCA used as a mechanism to avoid income tax and not as a true retirement arrangement, it will consider this as a salary deferral arrangement, with all amounts contributed becoming taxable immediately in the hands of the RCA beneficiary.

Sale of the Assets of a Business

Many business owners hope that they will be able to sell the shares of their business to someone else, but they often have no choice but to sell the assets of the business instead. When this occurs, the amount paid on the purchase is revenue to the company. This can lead to a very large tax bill in the form of corporate income tax, and possibly employer health tax, and personal income tax on the payment of a bonus or dividends.

In this case, an RCA is an ideal strategy. A large contribution to an RCA can vastly offset revenue. This way, you can defer all the proceeds of the sale of the assets of the business and make them available as a source of retirement income. The RCA can then pay income over, say, a period of ten years. The end result is that the business owner would pay much lower income tax in total. In many cases, this strategy will save hundreds of thousands of dollars.

Shortcomings of RCAs

The main shortcoming of RCAs is that only half of the assets will be invested. This is because half the contributions go to the RCA investment account and the other half is on deposit with the CRA in the refundable tax account.

You can overcome this disadvantage in two ways. First, achieving deferral of investment income in the RCA trust account will allow for greater growth of the assets. Second, it may be best to use up the RCA assets first during the few years of retirement and maximize the tax-deferred growth of the RRSP as late as possible, which would be at the end of the year in which the person reaches age seventy-one. This will compensate significantly for the absence of investment income of the refundable tax account.

Another shortcoming is that amounts paid out from an RCA are not eligible for the new pension income-splitting rules introduced in 2007 by the Government of Canada. This will be less of a factor if the surviving spouse will receive most of the income while in a lower tax bracket.

If the RCA is not carefully structured as a true retirement plan, or if the pension benefit formula is too generous compared to what is offered in registered pension plans, the CRA will deem the arrangement to be a salary deferral arrangement. The CRA is vague and there are few written rules, so it is best to adhere to the pension design that they publicly state to be acceptable. However, the CRA has publicly stated that their reasonability test is that the plan terms are set out in writing and an actuary certifies the plan's obligations.

Moreover, if the employee remuneration changes after setting up an RCA, the CRA may see the arrangement as a disguised salary deferral arrangement. For example, if an employee has a history of receiving an income of $400,000, but this gets reduced to $300,000 from the time the RCA is put in place, the CRA may question this. One approach that appears acceptable is to base the RCA pension on base salary, not base salary plus bonus, and not reduce the base salary to fund the RCA.

The RCA is a powerful strategy for business owners and incorporated professionals. They allow for large tax deductions to fund the retirement security of the business owner in a creditor-proof trust. At retirement, in many cases, personal income taxes will be lower, reducing the overall tax paid.

If it is the objective of the business owner to move out of Canada at retirement, the withholding tax on pension payments or lump sums will be lower, depending on the tax treaty, but it will be approximately 15% on installment payments and 25% on lump sums.

RCAs are able to solve many problems that business

owners face as they start thinking about retirement, including:

- Implementing a strategy for business succession planning and the sale or transition of the business at retirement
- Transferring assets tax-free from the business;
- Addressing the inadequacy of present and future RRSP limits;
- Creating a lifetime income to maintain a standard of living;
- Providing the peace of mind of knowing there is an ongoing source of income; and
- Providing a survivor income to the spouse and estate after business owner's death.

The RCA achieves a dramatic reduction in corporate income tax, a significant increase in net worth with tax-deferral, an attractive alternative to paying a taxable bonus, and an opportunity to transfer cash out of the company.

The following chart shows how the money flows between the company, RCA trust account, refundable trust account (RTA) with the CRA, and ultimately to the RCA beneficiary.

Retirement Compensation Arrangement

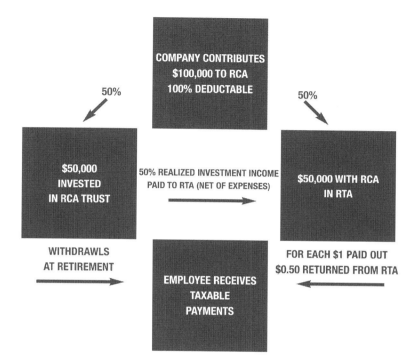

RCA Facts at a Glance

Contributions to RCA Trust and Refundable Tax Account (RTA)

- Deposited RCA contributions are in a trust (i.e. assets are separate from the company and protected from creditors).
- Contributions to an RCA are 100% deductible to the company and not taxable to the employee until paid out.
- 50% of contributions go to the RCA trust account.
- 50% of contributions go to the CRA in an RTA—amounts in the RTA earn 0%.
- Each year, 50% of realized investment income (interest, dividends, and realized capital gains) LESS expenses and

distributions is remitted to or refunded from the RTA.

- For each dollar paid out as a distribution from the RCA, $0.50 is paid back from RTA account until balance in the RTA is $0.
- There are no limits on contributions and retirement benefits; the only requirement is that contributions and benefits be reasonable based on employee's service and earnings.
- At retirement, termination of employment, or death, the company may hand over administration to the beneficiary of the trust.

RCA Distributions
- Are payable at termination of employment (loss of office), retirement, or death.
- On death, funds may be paid to spouse as a lump sum or survivor pension, or paid to a beneficiary.
- Can be settled as a lifetime pension, in a lump sum, or over a number of years.

Funding
- There are no funding requirements: complete contribution flexibility.
- Pension promise can be increased or decreased by amending plan terms.
- Tax-exempt life insurance or corporate class mutual funds provide full deferral of investment income in the RCA trust.

Benefits
- A typical pension promise would be 2% x Service x Best three-year average earnings.
- No maximum eligible earnings, unlike an IPP.
- Lower tax payable during retirement:
  - Tax reductions may continue in the future to match

other industrialized countries.

- In 2007, for federal income tax, the top marginal tax rate is 29% for income exceeding about $121,000.
- By law, tax brackets are indexed annually in line with inflation.
- If inflation remains at about 2.5%, the income threshold for the top marginal tax rate will be above $175,000 in fifteen years.

- Can defer starting distributions to maximize tax savings—for example, in the year after taking a large gain such as a company sale, or after depleting taxable non-registered assets or RRSP.

- If the beneficiary becomes a non-resident, withholding tax is generally 15% on installments and 25% on lump sums; in some cases, lower withholding applies depending on tax treaty.

- Taxpayer can still contribute to a personal RRSP.

- No heavy compliance, locking-in, or restricted payouts as with an IPP.

- No need to purchase an annuity or have a corporation after distributions begin.

- Beneficiaries of the RCA trust can be custodian (i.e. self-trusteed arrangement) or use a low-cost trust provider.

- Complete flexibility with respect to investments.

- Essentially, RCA contributions are fully tax-deductible; realized investment income is fully taxable.

Chapter 25
Retiring Allowances

In most cases, retiring allowances are paid to individuals on or after retirement to recognize long service, or sometimes paid to individuals as compensation for job loss due to things such as downsizing, restructuring, or other events. Whether the retirement or job loss is voluntary or involuntarily, the retiring allowance is generally considered termination pay. And although payments for sick leave are usually classified as employment income, if they are received on or after retirement, they usually qualify as a retiring allowance.

Retiring allowances have an advantage of being eligible for transfer to an RRSP without affecting the RRSP deduction limit and without being taxed. For funds to be eligible for transfer into an RRSP, you must be the RRSP owner and contributor. Spousal plans would therefore not qualify, and you would not be allowed to transfer funds into these types of plans.

The maximum amount of retiring allowance eligible for transfer into RRSPs or other registered plans on a tax-deferred basis is calculated based on the following combination:

- $2,000 per year of service with an employer prior to 1996; and
- An additional $1,500 per year of service prior to 1989 in which the employer pension plan or deferred profit-sharing plan contributions have not been vested.

You can handle the non-eligible amount of the retiring allowance, which is the amount in excess of the eligible amount, in the following way:

- Funds can be transferred as a contribution without withholding tax, assuming your employer is satisfied that you can use the full amount of transferred funds as an RRSP contribution.

- A contribution can be made to an RRSP or spousal RRSP, whereby you would include the non-eligible amount as income for tax purposes; you would, however, receive an offsetting deduction on the amount contributed to your spouse's RRSP.

In some cases of involuntary job loss, legal action is sought. If an individual has to obtain legal counsel to collect a retiring allowance, they can then deduct any legal expenses. The maximum deduction is based on the retiring allowance received and included as income minus any amount transferred to the individual's RRSP. In situations where you receive a retiring allowance over several years, it is important to note that the legal expenses incurred can be carried forward and used in any of the next seven taxation years.

Let's look at an example. Mark started work at Mac Food Distribution Company in 1980 and was recently laid off because of the company's losing of a major contract. The company did not have a registered pension plan, nor did it have a deferred profit-sharing plan. Mark received $52,000 as termination pay and an additional $3,000 for unused sick leave.

Termination pay	$52,000
Unused sick leave credit	$ 3,000
Total retiring allowance	$55,000
16 years of employment prior to 1996 @	
$2,000 per year	$32,000
9 years of employment prior to 1989 @	
$1,500 per year	$13,500
Total eligible for transfer to an RRSP	$45,500

Mark would be able to transfer $45,500 to an RRSP. The remaining $6,500 of the retiring allowance would be taxable unless Mark had unused RRSP contribution room. If this is the case, he can elect to transfer the funds into the RRSP, assuming his employer is satisfied with the information provided. He can elect to pay tax on the $6,500 and transfer the net proceeds to either his RRSP or a spousal RRSP. If Mark does not have RRSP contribution room, he can receive the funds, which would then be taxed.

Chapter 26
Registered Retirement Income Funds (RRIFs)

Although Registered Retirement Income Funds (RRIFs) are not the only option for maturing an RRSP, it is the one that provides the most flexibility and has many advantages over the many forms of annuities available.

RRSPs must be matured before December 31st of the year in which the annuitant turns seventy-one. The age limit was increased from sixty-nine to seventy-one in the latest federal budget.

There are three options for an RRSP at maturity:
1. Collapse the RRSP and receive a lump-sum payment.
2. Transfer the RRSP into an annuity.
3. Transfer the funds from the RRSP into a RRIF, whereby periodic income is paid out either monthly, quarterly, semi-annually, or annually.

Most Canadians realize that collapsing an RRSP and paying taxes on the full proceeds is not the most tax-effective way to structure retirement finances. Most people will transfer their funds to RRIFs because of the numerous advantages they provide, including:
- Flexibility in the type of investments: You can hold bonds, mutual funds, stocks, and other types of investments within an RRIF account.

- The annuitant can make withdrawals above the minimum amounts if required in any given year, although minimum withdrawals have to be made by the end of the year in which they turn seventy-two.
- Amounts withdrawn from the plan are usually a percentage of the value of the plan, therefore creating an asset that can be left for named beneficiaries.

Minimum amounts must be paid to individuals from each RRIF account held. This amount is included as taxable income. The minimum amount paid is a percentage based on your age and the value of the plan at the beginning of each year. For RRIFs established before 1992, a different formula is used; these are typically classified as "qualifying RRIFs."

Minimum Annual Withdrawals As a % of RRIF Assets

Age	RRIF	Qualifying RRIF
71	7.38%	5.26%
72	7.48%	5.56%
73	7.59%	5.88%
74	7.71%	6.25%
75	7.85%	6.67%
76	7.99%	7.14%
77	8.15%	7.69%
78	8.33%	8.33%
79	8.53%	8.53%
80	8.75%	8.75%
81	8.99%	8.99%
82	9.27%	9.27%
83	9.58%	9.58%
84	9.93%	9.93%
85	10.33%	10.33%
86	10.79%	10.79%

87	11.33%	11.33%
88	11.96%	11.96%
89	12.71%	12.71%
90	13.62%	13.62%
91	14.73%	14.73%
92	16.12%	16.12%
93	17.92%	17.92%
94*	20.00%	20.00%

*20% minimum withdrawal for individuals 94 years of age or older

Although the RRIF is established in the year an individual turns seventy-one years of age, the actual age with which the RRIF payment is calculated can be either the annuitant's or the annuitant's spouse's.

Other things to consider:
- You may contribute to your RRSPs in the year you turn seventy-one if you have earned income. The deadline for the final contribution is December 31st, as the normal sixty-day extension does not apply.
- If you are planning to convert your RRSP to an RRIF, you should consult with your advisor well ahead of the December 31st deadline. Payments do not have to start until the following year; therefore, there are no disadvantages to converting early in the year.
- Spousal contributions can still be continued after the age of seventy-one as long as you have earned income and your spouse is seventy-one years of age or younger.
- In the year the RRIF is established, there is no minimum withdrawal required.
- If you want to estimate your minimum RRIF payment, many financial calculators are available on the Internet.
- Consolidation of RRSP plans is usually recommended

when you have to convert your assets over to an RRIF. The transferring of an RRSP and opening of the RRIF account is a simple process. Ask your financial advisor to cover any transfer fees if they are going to benefit from your added business.

Chapter 27

Probate and Estate Taxation on Death

No government in Canada currently imposes direct estate taxes upon death. However, most estates and beneficiaries will feel the direct impact of taxation. While planning can be done to avoid and minimize taxation, such as naming a spouse as a beneficiary on an RRSP or RRIF, proper and comprehensive planning needs to be done to ensure estates can minimize probate fees (and in some cases eliminate them totally), resulting in thousands of dollars in savings.

When an individual dies, the probate process helps ensure that the will of the deceased is authentic—it also proves it is the individual's last and final will. Banks, financial institutions, investment brokerage firms, and even government agencies such as the Insurance Corporation of British Columbia (ICBC) or the Land Title office in most cases require probated wills, as this ensures they are dealing with an executor who is the final representative of the deceased.

Probate fees vary province to province and are based on the value of the deceased's assets that will pass through the estate. A reduction of debt associated with an asset passing through probate, such as a mortgage, is taken into consideration in some cases.

The following tables summarize current probate fees province to province:

Province	Value of Probate Assets	Fee Schedule
Alberta	Under $10,000	$25
	$10,000 to $24,999	$100
	$25,000 to 124,999	$200
	$125,000 to 249,999	$300
	$250,000 and over	$400
	*Alberta has maximum probate fess of $400	
British Columbia	Under $10,000	$0
	$10,001 to $25,000	$208
	$25,001 to $50,000	$6 for each $1,000
	$50,001 and over	$6/1,000 for amount between $25,001 and $50,000 and $14 for each $1,000 over $50,000
Manitoba	Under $10,000	$50
	$10,000 and over	$6 for every $1,000 over $10,000
New Brunswick	$1 and over	$5 for each $1,000
Newfoundland	Under $1,000	$85
	Over $1,000	$85 plus $5 per every $1,000 *Plus a $50 charge for the Order of the Court
Northwest Territories	Under $10,000	$25
	$10,000 to $25,000	$100
	$25,001 to $125,000	$200
	$125,001 to $250,000	$300
	Over $250,000	$400

Province	Value of Probate Assets	Fee Schedule
Nova Scotia	Under $10,000	$70
	$10,000 to $25,000	$176
	$25,001 to $50,000	$293
	$50,001 to $100,000	$820
	$100,000 and over	$820 plus $13.85 for every $1,000 over $100,000
Ontario	Up to $50,000	$5 for every $1,000
	Over $50,000	$5 for every $1,000 on the first $50,000 and $15 per $1,000 on amounts over $50,000
Prince Edward Island	Up to $10,000	$50
	$10,001 to $25,000	$100
	$25,001 to $50,000	$200
	$50,001 to $100,000	$400
	$100,001 and over	$400 plus $4 for each $1,000 over $100,000
		*additional 0.20% closing fee
Quebec		$65 for non-notarial wills
		$0 for notarial wills
Saskatchewan	$ Any amount	$7 on each $1,000
Yukon	Up to $25,000	No fee payable
	Over $25,000	$140

Strategies to Avoid Probate Fees

Proper and comprehensive planning can reduce or sometimes eliminate probate fees, especially when an estate passes between spouses. While it is difficult to eliminate probate fees when estates are passed between generations, the fees can be minimized.

To avoid or reduce probate fees, here are some things to consider:

Invest in Estate-Friendly Investments

Although many investments appear to be the same, there are added benefits with certain types of investment products offered through insurance companies. Investment products, including guaranteed investment certificates (GICs) and segregated mutual funds (which are also known as guaranteed investment funds), provide unique estate advantages, as named beneficiaries can be established on these. Since insurance investment products have named beneficiaries, the assets pass directly to the beneficiary and do not form a part of the deceased's estate, thereby bypassing probate.

Gifts Prior to Death

Assets can be given away prior to death to avoid probate. You should consider whether you are comfortable with giving up control of your assets prior to death. In addition, you should consider that if the market value of a gift is greater than the cost, the gain might be subject to tax. If you are uncomfortable with giving up control of your assets during your lifetime, you can establish an inter-vivos trust.

Establish an Inter-Vivos Trust

These types of trusts are set up during your lifetime. The trust is set up with you (the donor) giving or transferring your assets to the trust for the benefit of a named beneficiary or beneficiaries. Trustees then manage the assets within the trust for the benefit of the beneficiaries. By giving the assets to the trust during your lifetime, you no longer own the assets; you can, however, be a trustee yourself if you wish to have some control over the assets.

Joint Tenancy

Property owned jointly passes automatically by right of survivorship to the surviving joint owner and therefore is not part of the estate and bypasses probate. Although owning assets jointly has many advantages, joint tenancy can have disadvantages, which can include losing control of the assets. Many people aren't comfortable with the idea of registering investment portfolios jointly with their children or other individuals. The same can be said of real estate, businesses, and other assets.

Corporate Debt

You may deduct mortgage debts from the value of the property in an estate, but other types of debt are not used when calculating the value of an estate.

If you purchase an asset with borrowed money, such as an unsecured line of credit, transferring the asset along with the debt to a limited company will reduce the value of an estate and therefore the amount of probate fees. In this situation, you would no longer own the asset, the corporation would. While the company's shares form part of the estate and would be subject to probate fees, the value of the shares would take into consideration the value of the debt.

Named Beneficiaries

Beneficiaries named under plans such as RRSPs, RRIFs, locked-in RRSPs, LIFs, and other types of pensions along with insurance policies and insurance company investment products allow for proceeds to bypass the probate process.

Naming a beneficiary other than the estate can therefore save substantial amounts of probate fees.

Property Transferred to a Trust

An asset held within a trust is not considered part of an estate. You can therefore create a trust to hold property on your behalf, with provisions for the distribution of income or capital to be made directly to the named beneficiaries. Although transferring assets to a trust will reduce probateable assets, the drawback is that the cost of creating and administering the trust could be high. In addition, assets within the trust are taxed at higher rates than they would be if you held them. Two common types of trusts are joint spousal trusts and alter-ego trusts.

Consider the following example to see how a spousal trust can work. If Dave leaves property to a spousal trust for the benefit of his wife, Sheila, during her lifetime, Sheila can use the trust property during her lifetime. In addition to using the property, Sheila would be allowed to spend the income from the trust. In this case, where a spousal trust is used, the property is not in Sheila's name, as it is held in the trust. When Sheila dies, the assets would directly pass to the beneficiaries of the trust without being included in Sheila's estate. In addition to these potential benefits, another advantage is that during her lifetime, Sheila and the trust are treated as separate taxpayers and this can result in lower income taxes being paid compared to having all the assets and income being held by one taxpayer.

Chapter 28
Offshore Investing

More and more investors are seeking information on offshore investing, as they wish to avoid paying taxes or minimize their tax burden on their Canadian dollars abroad.

You should consider several things before you send your money to a potential tax haven in an offshore jurisdiction. Canada has some of the most diligent securities and banking regulatory agencies in the world. In addition to the regulatory protection, investors have the benefits of the Canadian Investor Protection Fund (CIPF) should the broker go bankrupt. The Canadian system also offers investors some potential recourse in civil court if they feel they have been financially harmed. In offshore jurisdictions, similar civil actions would be very difficult or next to impossible to perform. If you send your money offshore, be prepared to forego the protections offered by the provincial securities commissions and the Canadian banking system.

Although Canadian residents must declare worldwide income according to the CRA and the Government of Canada, investors can use legal methods in creating offshore structures that are completely legal in Canada and hence reduce their taxable liabilities.

International business companies (IBCs) offer a viable option and can possibly provide an effective way to shelter assets from Canadian tax. In order for an IBC to be considered a sound tax shelter, the CRA requires that there must be some bona fide purpose other than tax avoidance for establishing one. If structured properly and given the right circumstances, trusts can be established for individuals immigrating to Canada or emigrating from Canada. These trusts, especially the immigration trust, are covered in chapter 29, which focuses on immigration trusts.

When discussing the benefits of offshore investing, we specifically mean creating a new entity offshore. Offshore investing can be extremely simple in terms of the asset selection. The investments can be in simple products such as high-interest savings accounts or term deposits, bonds, stocks, or commodities.

Structured properly with the right professionals, offshore investing can reduce investment tax to virtually zero and is considered a very solid estate-planning strategy. Offshore assets do not have to flow through probate after death, and while alive, you do not have to worry about the possibility of losing assets due to lawsuits, divorces, or other factors. Offshore investing creditor-proofs your assets.

Consider offshore investments if you are concerned about reducing your tax burden, interested in increasing your privacy, wish to creditor-proof your assets, or looking for higher potential returns on your investments.

Chapter 29
Immigration Trusts

New immigrants to Canada may shelter their foreign income for a period of up to five years by establishing a foreign trust outside of Canada.

A Canadian tax resident is subject to Canadian tax on their worldwide income from the time they obtain Canadian residency. Foreigners become Canadian residents for tax purposes if they stay more than 183 days in the jurisdiction within any taxation year.

An immigration trust can help preserve and enhance an immigrant's wealth by providing tax deferral for a period of up to five years. Generally, the trust receives the benefits of tax exemption on all of its income, including interest, dividends, and capital gains. The trust can be established before the immigrant becomes a resident of Canada and should be wound down before the expiration of the five-year period.

The trust must be irrevocable for the five-year period. Revocable trusts, which allow the property to revert to the settler or to individuals determined by the settler, will not provide the desired taxation shelter.

Immigration trusts were originally intended to allow executives from foreign multinational corporations who were temporarily transferred to Canada to leave their investments in offshore tax havens. They are simply non-resident trusts established in foreign tax jurisdictions that hold foreign investment assets. The trust itself is an arrangement between three parties:

1. The settler, who is typically a non-Canadian resident who creates the trust and funds the initial contribution or investment;
2. The trustee, who is typically an offshore trust company or a non-Canadian resident who manages the investments for the benefit of the recipients; and
3. The beneficiaries, normally the immigrating parties who are the recipients of the trust.

An immigration trust is normally established before an individual becomes a resident of Canada. It can, however, be done at any time within the first five years of Canadian residency. Since the five-year period starts at the time an individual establishes Canadian residency, the tax-free benefits of the income and capital gains is maximized when the immigration trust is set up before becoming a resident of Canada. The income and capital gains earned from the investments in the trust, along with the capital in the trust, may be distributed to the named beneficiaries in future years without incurring any Canadian income tax.

Immigration trusts are generally U.S.-dollar-denominated trusts. The tax savings over a five-year period can be substantial. The larger the trust, the larger the tax savings. Given the significant costs of creating and administering an immigration trust, an immigrant should have in excess of U.S.$500,000 for this strategy to be considered.

If you wish to consider immigration trusts, you should deal with knowledgeable and reputable tax advisors, lawyers, and financial planners. Your team of experienced advisors will be able to review your personal situation and work with each other to provide you with a comprehensive range of products and services, including investment, custody, banking, and credit services. You should also consider the political and economic stability of the jurisdiction where the trust is being established.

Chapter 30

Become a Non-Resident: Stop Paying Income Taxes Completely

Interested in paying no tax? The one simple solution is becoming a non-resident of Canada. The Government of Canada taxes its residents, not its citizens. Many think that you must give up your citizenship to avoid taxes; however, this is not the case.

Becoming a non-resident is not that simple. The Canada Revenue Agency (CRA) developed a test to determine an individual's residency. One of their bulletins on this issue is called "Determination of an Individual's Residency Status." In summary, their primary test is to see whether individuals have ties with Canada. Some of the questions asked are:

- Do you have a dwelling?
- Do you have a spouse or common-law spouse who is staying in the country?
- Do you have dependents in the country?

The secondary test includes questions such as:

- Do you own any personal property in Canada, such as cars, furniture, or clothing?
- Do you have ties such as employment with a Canadian employer or are you actively involved in a Canadian business?
- Do you have securities accounts in Canada or registered accounts, bank accounts, or credit cards?
- Do you have a cottage in Canada?

- Do you have any memberships in Canadian unions or professional organizations?
- Do you have any Canadian social ties, such as memberships at fitness clubs or other recreational organizations?
- Do you have a Canadian driver's license?
- Do you have Canadian medical insurance?

If you feel the CRA considers you a resident, then you can start planning to change your current situation. Remember, as a non-resident, you can stay in Canada no more than 182 days per year. So individuals looking at retiring and spending time in the southern States or Mexico might want to consider this strategy.

Those hoping to become a non-resident are typically interested in sheltering future growth from capital gains taxes. You should always seek professional tax and accounting advice before becoming a non-resident because at the time of emigration, you are deemed to have disposed all of your capital property at a fair market value. This results in potential capital gains implications regardless of the country in which you reside and regardless of the tax treaty in place between Canada and the other country.

If you become a non-resident, it does not mean you cannot hold Canadian assets or investments. Non-residents are taxed through a withholding tax system in Canada. The basic Canadian withholding tax is 25%. This typically applies to investment income, dividends, some types of interest payments, certain pensions, certain types of royalties, rental income, and income from a trust. If a tax treaty exists between Canada and the other country, the withholding tax can be reduced to 15% and sometimes less. The withholding tax is withheld from the gross payment.

There are excellent benefits to becoming a non-resident. It is a strategy often contemplated by the very affluent as a way to reduce or eliminate taxes on investment income and growth in assets or trusts. For example, non-residents of Canada who invest in Government of Canada bonds or provincial bonds will pay no withholding tax on their investments.

Although many benefits exist in becoming a non-resident, there is a stumbling block for those considering this tax-planning strategy. Canada has imposed an exit tax whereby an individual is deemed to have disposed certain capital property at fair market value. The deemed disposition applies to all forms of property with the following exceptions:

- Canadian real estate that was already owned when residency in Canada was established if the residency did not exceed five years out of the last ten years;
- Property used in a business;
- Some pensions, including RRSPs and RRIFs;
- Stock options in certain cases; and
- Interest in some Canadian trusts.

The taxes incurred from the deemed disposition do not have to be paid right away in some cases. You are allowed to post security in the form of a bond, letter of credit, or mortgage or bank guarantee to cover the tax liability until the asset is actually sold.

In addition to individuals being subject to exit rules, corporations leaving Canada are also subject to these rules. A corporation is deemed to have disposed all of its property at fair market value. The corporation is then deemed to have distributed the net equity.

Let us consider the following example of a client looking to become a non-resident of Canada. Gary and Leanne have accumulated a net worth of over $2,000,000 and are contemplating moving to Mexico. Their assets are comprised as follows:

- Principal residence of $450,000;
- RRSPs totalling a combined $350,000;

- Non-registered investments totalling $600,000; and
- Farm property qualified under CRA rules valued at $600,000, which they purchased for $220,000 ten years ago.

Assuming they wish to proceed with becoming non-residents, Gary and Leanne can use proper planning to ensure no significant tax liabilities are created. They are able to sell their principal residence and not pay capital gains tax, as taxes are not payable on the sale of principal residences. In addition, their RRSPs are not disposed of for tax purposes because they are exempt from the property classification for deemed dispositions. The income taken out of the RRSP, or the income taken out of the RRIF if the RRSP is rolled over into an RRIF, would be subject to Canadian withholding tax at a rate between 15% and 25%, depending on whether the funds were withdrawn on a regular basis as a period pension payment or as a lump-sum payment.

Their non-registered portfolio would attract a deemed disposition. If Gary and Leanne are conservative investors, however, they might benefit from the fact that there is no withholding tax should they invest their non-registered funds into a series of Government of Canada or provincial bonds. Their farm property would realize a $380,000 capital gain. However, if Gary and Leanne did not use their capital gains exemption of $500,000, they would take steps to crystallize the gain before emigrating.

There are many advantages of being taxed as a non-resident of Canada, but only a small number of people will actually contemplate becoming one. Always seek professional tax and legal advice before becoming a non-resident.

Chapter 31

What Your Advisor Should Tell You and What Questions You Should Ask

Your advisor should tell you what types of products and services to which they have access. The reality is that most advisors don't. For example, most financial advisors who work for the banks are usually licensed by the Mutual Fund Dealers Association (MFDA) and can therefore only offer you mutual fund investments and GICs. The mutual funds are typically the banks' own mutual funds and sometimes mutual fund wrap accounts with third-party funds. Some banks allow their advisors to sell and promote a select portfolio of third-party funds; however, in reality, they very rarely actually promote them for a variety of reasons. Many advisors do not have access to bonds, nor can they provide advice on stocks, hedge funds, tax shelters such as flow-through shares, Individual Pension Plans, options, and other investment products.

Ask your advisor what types of products they can sell you. Ask them how they are compensated to sell each of the products. If they tell you they can offer you mutual funds from a variety of fund companies, ask which fund companies and if they are compensated the same way for each of them. Ask the advisors if they can provide advice on tax shelters such as flow-through investments. Ask for access to other products such as GICs from other banks and high-interest savings accounts.

The bottom line is that you should know what products

are available to you. Below is a list of questions you should ask your financial advisor:

1. Will I have access to GICs from a variety of financial institutions, and if so, which ones?
2. Are bonds available with you? Government, provincial, and corporate bonds?

   MFDA licensed companies are not licensed to sell and advise on any bond offerings (e.g. Province of Ontario Bonds).

   MFDA licensed companies who hold a limited market dealer license by the Ontario Securities Commission are licensed to sell and advise on government and provincial bonds.

   IDA licensed advisors are able to offer government, provincial, and corporate bonds.
3. Which mutual fund companies will I have access to? Are you compensated the same way regardless of which mutual funds I purchase?

   Some companies only offer a select number of mutual funds. Ensure you have access to a large selection of funds, including companies such as Sprott Asset Management, Sceptre Investment Counsel, Chou, Northwest, and the larger well-known ones such as AIM Trimark, Franklin Templeton, and GGOF.
4. How do you select the mutual funds you recommend?

   Ensure your advisor is knowledgeable about the investment markets. It is extremely easy to pick last year's top performing funds. Ensure the advisor describes the value and benefit of each fund.
5. Do you provide your clients with access to hedge funds?

   Hedge funds are becoming extremely popular and can reduce risk in your investment portfolio. Although you may not want hedge funds in your portfolio, your advisor should be familiar with them and recognize the benefits of adding some hedge-type funds into investor portfolios.

6. Do you provide your clients with access to options?

    Options strategies can both increase returns and limit risk for very sophisticated investors.

7. Do you provide your clients with access to individual stocks? If so, how do you determine which ones have good potential? What commission do you charge for stock trades?

8. How are you compensated? And do you receive additional income or bonuses for hitting any sales targets for any one specific investment you recommend?

    Most advisors are compensated on a commission basis. In addition, some commissioned advisors are paid increased bonuses for hitting certain levels in assets for certain products. More specifically, many are paid at high commission and/or bonus levels if a certain portion of there sales are in a certain class of products that are generally bigger revenue generators for the bank.

9. Do you provide advice on tax shelters other than RRSPs? Are you licensed to offer flow-through securities?

    If your income is in excess of $80,000 or if you anticipate not needing the income from your registered plans at retirement, you might want to discuss flow-through securities with your advisor.

10. Do you have access to segregated funds? If so, from which companies?

    If you are a business owner or are self-employed, you might want to consider segregated funds, so ask your advisor if they are licensed to sell them. If they are, ask if they represent numerous big insurance companies such as AIG, Standard Life, Manulife, and some of the others.

11. Are you licensed to sell life insurance?

    Although you may not need life insurance, it is good to receive an evaluation to ensure you are sufficiently covered. Also, you may at some point want to discuss other forms of insurance such as critical illness and disability insurance.

Types of Advisors and Accounts

Independent Financial Planners

The number of independent financial planners in Canada is growing at a rapid pace. This type of financial professional typically deals with investment portfolios ranging in size from $25,000 to up to a few million dollars, depending on the experience of the advisor. Many of these advisors have access to some or many of the products mentioned in this book, depending on the organization where they work and the type of license they hold. Independent advisors are under the same rules and regulations as the advisors working for some of the largest organizations. They usually hold client accounts at financial institutions such as MRS Trust, B2B Trust, and Canadian Western Trust. MRS Trust, for example, administers over $4 billion dollars for over 250,000 account holders.

Investment Counsellors

Many individuals profess the need to deal with experienced investment counsellors if investible assets total in excess of $1,000,000. Some money managers will take accounts in the range of $500,000. Those who prefer dealing with investment counsellors should recognize that individual stocks and bonds are purchased and sold similar to the way many brokers would handle their accounts. The difference typically lies with the fact that many accounts are opened on a discretionary basis. Clients grant their counsellors with the ability to buy and sell in their accounts according to their investment policy statement and the investment objectives in the account. Investment counsellors typically charge clients a certain percentage based on assets. The fees are typically between 1% and 1.5% of the value of the account. Clients often also pay additional trading charges and minimal custodial and administration charges.

TAL, Davis Rae, Cumberland Asset Management, and Mulvihill Capital are just a few of the companies around.

Brokerage Accounts

For decades, many investors would rely on the expertise of their stockbrokers to manage their financial affairs. Richardson Greenshields, Burns Fry, Midland Walwyn were typical brokerage companies. Canada's major banks have purchased many of the well-established independent brokerage companies. RBC Dominion Securities, or RBC Investments as it is also known, is RBC's full-service brokerage company. CIBC Wood Gundy, BMO Nesbitt Burns, ScotiaMcLeod are also bank-owned brokerage companies.

The reality is, in today's age and financial environment, the traditional stockbroker has in essence changed a great deal. Although many advisors still perceive themselves as stockbrokers, many now simply refer to themselves as financial planners or investment advisors. More and more advisors and companies are using in-house investment portfolios such as RBC Sovereign Investment Program and many others.

Brokerage fees are typically substantial in comparison to discount brokerage fees. In addition to offering commission-based structures, where investors pay commissions per transaction, more and more prefer to offer fee-based accounts, where a client pays a certain amount per year based on assets, which is typically a percentage ranging from 1.0% to 2.5% of the value of the account. In my view, this is a decent way to go if a client chooses to do a lot of individual equity trading, but for most clients who choose to be in a balanced portfolio, there is no need to pay a broker a 2% fee to hold Government of Canada bonds.

Investment advisors at these companies typically will not look at accounts under $250,000, and many have even higher minimum thresholds. The lower the amount, the lower the level of service you will likely receive from your advisor, and it is entirely likely that the account will actually be handed over to a junior. With brokerage accounts, you rely on the advice of the individual advisor, yet you have the ultimate say in whether anything is bought or sold in your account.

Self-Directed Accounts

These accounts had basically grown to absurd numbers over the '90s, as more and more day traders and do-it-yourselfers thought they could do better than their advisors. Many of them learned valuable and expensive lessons in that investing is not an area where you want to learn as you go. Although individuals made substantial amounts of money buying and selling stocks on their own, especially during the tech bubble, many saw their vast fortunes disappear virtually overnight.

Today, investors use self-directed accounts to both trade stocks over the short term and buy investments over the long term. As opposed to dealing with a bank financial advisor, they open self-directed accounts, where they can hold bonds, stocks, and mutual funds from all the banks all in one account. Self-directed investors pay smaller commissions than those paid while dealing with a full-service brokerage firm because they do not receive any advice on what they should buy. It is really a do-it-yourself platform.

Individuals looking for self-directed accounts should look at TD Waterhouse, BMO Investorline, Scotia Direct Trading, RBC Action Direct, and a few others. The service is good, as are the product lines; however, they do not provide any advice whatsoever. Many independent planners offer their clients access to many of the above-mentioned products and services, with value-added expertise and advice, and with the same commission structure as the discount brokers.

Banks, Trust Companies, and Credit Unions

Banks, trust companies, and credit unions provide access to a variety of products and services. Although a large percentage of investors deal with financial advisors or other bankers, most Canadians see the value and benefit of dealing with a truly unbiased financial service organization. When you think about it logically, do you really think an individual at one Canadian bank would recommend a product from another Canadian bank? For example, if you deal at RBC and walk into one of their branches, do you think they would recommend a CIBC mutual fund? Although they are starting to provide their advisors with access to a broader line of products and services from other financial institutions, they have a long way to go.

The bottom line is that banks will continue to have a strong hold on the financial planning marketplace. It's not, however, due to their expertise in the branches or superior products. It's because of the convenience and the perceived safety of dealing with big banks. Also, in terms of building long-standing relationships with a banker, the turnover is usually high and the probability of your account manager or financial advisor being there in five years is unlikely.

Appendix 1

Marginal Tax Rate Tables

Marginal Tax Rates for 2007 as of July 1, 2007
Alberta

2007 Taxable Income	Interest and Other Income	Capital Gains	Canadian Small Business Dividends	Eligible Dividends
Up to $8,929	-	-	-	-
Over $8,929 up to $15,435	15.50%	7.75%	2.71%	-5.02%
$15,436 up to $37,178	25.50%	12.75%	8.33%	-2.12%
$37,179 up to $74,356	32.00%	16.00%	16.45%	7.30%
$74,357 up to $120,887	36.00%	18.00%	21.45%	13.10%
$120,888 and over	39.00%	19.50%	25.20%	17.45%

Rates are federal, provincial, and territorial marginal tax rates combined. The rates include all surtaxes.

Assumption made that credits claimed are the basic personal amount and the low income tax reduction if applicable.

Eligible dividends are 1) those paid by Canadian public corporations and other corporations that are not CCPCs and are subject to general federal corporate tax rates and 2) income from CCPCs that is not investment income and is subject to general federal corporate tax rates.

Marginal Tax Rates for 2007 as of July 1, 2007
British Columbia

2007 Taxable Income	Interest and Other Income	Capital Gains	Canadian Small Business Dividends	Eligible Dividends
Up to $8,929	-	-	-	-
Over $8,929 up to $15,606	15.50%	7.75%	2.71%	-5.02%
$15,607 up to $16,645	21.20%	10.60%	3.46%	-13.14%
$16,646 up to $27,675	24.60%	12.30%	7.71%	-9.22%
$27,676 up to $34,397	21.20%	10.60%	3.46%	-14.15%
$34,398 up to $37,178	24.15%	12.08%	7.41%	-9.88%
$37,179 up to $68,794	30.65%	15.33%	15.26%	-0.46%
$68,795 up to $74,357	33.10%	16.55%	18.33%	3.10%
$74,358 up to $78,984	37.10%	18.55%	23.33%	8.90%
$78,985 up to $95,909	39.00%	19.50%	25.70%	11.65%
$95,910 up to $120,887	40.70%	20.35%	27.83%	14.12%
$120,888 and over	43.70%	21.85%	31.58%	18.47%

Rates are federal, provincial, and territorial marginal tax rates combined. The rates include all surtaxes.

Assumption made that credits claimed are the basic personal amount and the low income tax reduction if applicable.

Eligible dividends are 1) those paid by Canadian public corporations and other corporations that are not CCPCs and are subject to general federal corporate tax rates and 2) income from CCPCs that is not investment income and is subject to general federal corporate tax rates.

Marginal Tax Rates for 2007 as of July 1, 2007
Manitoba

2007 Taxable Income	Interest and Other Income	Capital Gains	Canadian Small Business Dividends	Eligible Dividends
Up to $8,929	-	-	-	-
Over $8,929 up to $9,066	15.50%	7.75%	2.71%	-5.02%
$9,067 up to $22,500	27.40%	13.70%	11.50%	-3.71%
$22,501 up to $30,545	26.40%	13.20%	10.25%	-5.16%
$30,545 up to $37,178	28.50%	14.25%	12.87%	-2.12%
$37,179 up to $65,000	35.00%	17.50%	20.99%	7.30%
$65,001 up to $74,357	39.40%	19.70%	26.49%	13.68%
$74,358 up to $120,887	43.40%	21.70%	31.49%	19.48%
$120,888 and over	46.40%	23.20%	35.24%	23.83%

Rates are federal, provincial, and territorial marginal tax rates combined. The rates include all surtaxes.

Assumption made that credits claimed are the basic personal amount and the low income tax reduction if applicable.

Eligible dividends are 1) those paid by Canadian public corporations and other corporations that are not CCPCs and are subject to general federal corporate tax rates and 2) income from CCPCs that is not investment income and is subject to general federal corporate tax rates.

Marginal Tax Rates for 2007 as of July 1, 2007
New Brunswick

2007 Taxable Income	Interest and Other Income	Capital Gains	Canadian Small Business Dividends	Eligible Dividends
Up to $8,929	-	-	-	-
Over $8,929 up to $13,511	15.50%	7.75%	2.71%	-5.02%
$13,512 up to $13,750	25.62%	12.81%	10.73%	1.96%
$13,751 up to $24,419	30.62%	15.31%	16.98%	9.21%
$24,420 up to $34,186	25.62%	12.81%	10.73%	1.96%
$34,187 up to $37,178	30.98%	15.49%	17.43%	9.74%
$37,179 up to $68,374	37.48%	18.74%	25.55%	19.16%
$68,375 up to $74,357	38.80%	19.40%	27.20%	21.07%
$74,358 up to $111,161	42.80%	21.40%	32.20%	26.87%
$111,162 up to $120,887	43.95%	21.98%	33.64%	28.54%
$120,888 and over	46.95%	23.47%	37.39%	32.89%

Rates are federal, provincial, and territorial marginal tax rates combined. The rates include all surtaxes.

Assumption made that credits claimed are the basic personal amount and the low income tax reduction if applicable.

Eligible dividends are 1) those paid by Canadian public corporations and other corporations that are not CCPCs and are subject to general federal corporate tax rates and 2) income from CCPCs that is not investment income and is subject to general federal corporate tax rates.

Marginal Tax Rates for 2007 as of July 1, 2007
Newfoundland and Labrador

2007 Taxable Income	Interest and Other Income	Capital Gains	Canadian Small Business Dividends	Eligible Dividends
Up to $8,929	-	-	-	-
Over $8,929 up to $12,192	15.50%	7.75%	2.71%	-5.02%
$12,193 up to $16,645	24.20%	12.10%	7.34%	-2.04%
$13,000 up to $27,675	40.20%	20.10%	27.34%	21.16%
$15,601 up to $34,397	24.20%	12.10%	7.34%	-2.04%
$29,591 up to $37,178	29.30%	14.65%	13.71%	5.35%
$37,179 up to $68,794	35.80%	17.90%	21.83%	14.77%
$59,181 up to $74,357	38.50%	19.25%	25.21%	18.69%
$74,358 up to $78,984	42.50%	21.25%	30.21%	24.49%
$120,888 and over	45.50%	22.75%	33.96%	28.84%

Rates are federal, provincial, and territorial marginal tax rates combined. The rates include all surtaxes.

Assumption made that credits claimed are the basic personal amount and the low income tax reduction if applicable.

Eligible dividends are 1) those paid by Canadian public corporations and other corporations that are not CCPCs and are subject to general federal corporate tax rates and 2) income from CCPCs that is not investment income and is subject to general federal corporate tax rates.

Marginal Tax Rates for 2007 as of July 1, 2007
Northwest Territories

2007 Taxable Income	Interest and Other Income	Capital Gains	Canadian Small Business Dividends	Eligible Dividends
Up to $8,929	-	-	-	-
Over $8,929 up to $12,125	15.50%	7.75%	2.71%	-5.02%
$12,126 up to $35,315	21.40%	10.70%	2.59%	-13.14%
$35,316 up to $37,178	24.10%	12.05%	5.96%	-9.23%
$37,179 up to $70,631	30.60%	15.30%	14.08%	0.19%
$70,632 up to $74,356	34.20%	17.10%	18.58%	5.41%
$74,357 up to $114,830	38.20%	19.10%	23.58%	11.21%
$114,831 up to $120,887	40.05%	20.02%	25.89%	13.89%
$120,888 and over	43.05%	21.52%	29.64%	18.24%

Rates are federal, provincial, and territorial marginal tax rates combined. The rates include all surtaxes.

Assumption made that credits claimed are the basic personal amount and the low income tax reduction if applicable.

Eligible dividends are 1) those paid by Canadian public corporations and other corporations that are not CCPCs and are subject to general federal corporate tax rates and 2) income from CCPCs that is not investment income and is subject to general federal corporate tax rates.

Marginal Tax Rates for 2007 as of July 1, 2007
Nova Scotia

2007 Taxable Income	Interest and Other Income	Capital Gains	Canadian Small Business Dividends	Eligible Dividends
Up to $8,929	-	-	-	-
Over $8,929 up to $10,894	15.50%	7.75%	2.71%	-5.02%
$10,895 up to $14,999	24.29%	12.14%	4.07%	-3.66%
$15,000 up to $20,999	29.29%	14.65%	10.32%	2.59%
$21,000 up to $29,590	24.29%	12.14%	4.07%	-3.66%
$29,591 up to $37,178	30.45%	15.23%	11.77%	4.04%
$37,179 up to $59,180	36.95%	18.47%	19.89%	13.46%
$59,181 up to $74,357	38.67%	19.33%	22.04%	15.61%
$74,358 up to $80,973	42.67%	21.34%	27.04%	21.41%
$80,974 up to $93,000	44.34%	22.17%	28.17%	22.53%
$93,001 up to $120,887	45.25%	22.62%	29.31%	23.67%
$120,888 and over	48.25%	24.12%	33.05%	28.02%

Rates are federal, provincial, and territorial marginal tax rates combined. The rates include all surtaxes.

Assumption made that credits claimed are the basic personal amount and the low income tax reduction if applicable.

Eligible dividends are 1) those paid by Canadian public corporations and other corporations that are not CCPCs and are subject to general federal corporate tax rates and 2) income from CCPCs that is not investment income and is subject to general federal corporate tax rates.

Marginal Tax Rates for 2007 as of July 1, 2007
Nunavut

2007 Taxable Income	Interest and Other Income	Capital Gains	Canadian Small Business Dividends	Eligible Dividends
Up to $8,929	-	-	-	-
Over $8,929 up to $11,149	15.50%	7.75%	2.71%	-5.02%
$11,150 up to $37,178	19.50%	9.75%	2.71%	-5.02%
$37,179 up to $74,357	29.00%	14.50%	14.58%	8.15%
$74,358 up to $120,887	35.00%	17.50%	22.08%	16.45%
$120,888 and over	40.50%	20.25%	28.96%	23.93%

Rates are federal, provincial, and territorial marginal tax rates combined. The rates include all surtaxes.

Assumption made that credits claimed are the basic personal amount and the low income tax reduction if applicable.

Eligible dividends are 1) those paid by Canadian public corporations and other corporations that are not CCPCs and are subject to general federal corporate tax rates and 2) income from CCPCs that is not investment income and is subject to general federal corporate tax rates.

Marginal Tax Rates for 2007 as of July 1, 2007
Ontario

2007 Taxable Income	Interest and Other Income	Capital Gains	Canadian Small Business Dividends	Eligible Dividends
Up to $8,929	-	-	-	-
Over $8,929 up to $11,826	15.50%	7.75%	2.71%	-5.02%
$11,827 up to $15,100	27.60%	13.80%	5.01%	-6.92%
$15,101 up to $35,488	21.55%	10.78%	3.86%	-5.97%
$35,489 up to $37,178	24.65%	12.32%	7.74%	-1.47%
$37,179 up to $62,490	31.15%	15.58%	15.86%	7.95%
$62,491 up to $70,976	32.98%	16.49%	16.87%	8.66%
$70,977 up to $73,616	35.39%	17.70%	19.88%	12.15%
$73,617 up to $74,357	39.41%	19.70%	22.59%	14.48%
$74,358 up to $120,887	43.41%	21.70%	27.59%	20.28%
$120,888 and over	46.41%	23.20%	31.34%	24.64%

Rates are federal, provincial, and territorial marginal tax rates combined. The rates include all surtaxes.

Assumption made that credits claimed are the basic personal amount and the low income tax reduction if applicable.

Eligible dividends are 1) those paid by Canadian public corporations and other corporations that are not CCPCs and are subject to general federal corporate tax rates and 2) income from CCPCs that is not investment income and is subject to general federal corporate tax rates.

Marginal Tax Rates for 2007 as of July 1, 2007
Prince Edward Island

2007 Taxable Income	Interest and Other Income	Capital Gains	Canadian Small Business Dividends	Eligible Dividends
Up to $8,929	-	-	-	-
Over $8,929 up to $10,112	15.50%	7.75%	2.71%	-5.02%
$10,113 up to $14,999	25.30%	12.65%	5.33%	-2.40%
$15,000 up to $19,999	30.30%	15.15%	11.58%	3.85%
$20,000 up to $31,369	25.30%	12.65%	5.33%	-2.40%
$31,370 up to $37,178	29.30%	14.65%	10.33%	2.60%
$37,179 up to $62,739	35.80%	17.90%	18.45%	12.02%
$62,740 up to $74,357	40.37%	20.18%	23.21%	16.78%
$74,358 up to $120,887	44.37%	22.18%	28.20%	22.57%
$120,888 and over	47.37%	23.68%	31.96%	26.92%

Rates are federal, provincial, and territorial marginal tax rates combined. The rates include all surtaxes.

Assumption made that credits claimed are the basic personal amount and the low income tax reduction if applicable.

Eligible dividends are 1) those paid by Canadian public corporations and other corporations that are not CCPCs and are subject to general federal corporate tax rates and 2) income from CCPCs that is not investment income and is subject to general federal corporate tax rates.

Marginal Tax Rates for 2007 as of July 1, 2007 Quebec

2007 Taxable Income	Interest and Other Income	Capital Gains	Canadian Small Business Dividends	Eligible Dividends
Up to $8,929	-	-	-	-
Over $8,929 up to $12,185	12.94%	6.47%	2.26%	-4.19%
$12,186 up to $29,292	28.94%	14.47%	12.26%	1.76%
$29,293 up to $37,178	32.94%	16.47%	17.26%	7.55%
$37,179 up to $58,595	38.37%	19.19%	24.04%	15.41%
$58,596 up to $74,357	42.37%	21.19%	29.04%	21.21%
$74,358 up to $120,887	45.71%	22.85%	33.22%	26.06%
$120,888 and over	48.21%	24.10%	36.35%	29.69%

Rates are federal, provincial, and territorial marginal tax rates combined. The rates include all surtaxes.

Assumption made that credits claimed are the basic personal amount and the low income tax reduction if applicable.

Eligible dividends are 1) those paid by Canadian public corporations and other corporations that are not CCPCs and are subject to general federal corporate tax rates and 2) income from CCPCs that is not investment income and is subject to general federal corporate tax rates.

Marginal Tax Rates for 2007 as of July 1, 2007
Saskatchewan

2007 Taxable Income	Interest and Other Income	Capital Gains	Canadian Small Business Dividends	Eligible Dividends
Up to $8,778	-	-	-	-
Over $8,778 up to $8,929	11.00%	5.50%	6.25%	-
$8,930 up to $37,178	26.50%	13.25%	8.96%	-5.02%
$37,179 up to $38,406	33.00	16.50%	17.08%	4.40%
$38,407 up to $74,357	35.00%	17.50%	19.58%	7.30%
$74,358 up to $109,729	39.00%	19.50%	24.58%	13.10%
$109,730 up to $120,877	41.00%	20.50%	27.08%	16.00%
$120,888 and over	44.00%	22.00%	30.83%	20.35%

Rates are federal, provincial, and territorial marginal tax rates combined. The rates include all surtaxes.

Assumption made that credits claimed are the basic personal amount and the low income tax reduction if applicable.

Eligible dividends are 1) those paid by Canadian public corporations and other corporations that are not CCPCs and are subject to general federal corporate tax rates and 2) income from CCPCs that is not investment income and is subject to general federal corporate tax rates.

Marginal Tax Rates for 2007 as of July 1, 2007
Yukon

2007 Taxable Income	Interest and Other Income	Capital Gains	Canadian Small Business Dividends	Eligible Dividends
Up to $8,929	-	-	-	-
Over $8,929 up to $14,255	16.91%	8.45%	3.00%	-4.73%
$14,256 up to $14,999	22.54%	11.27%	4.17%	-3.56%
$15,000 up to $24,999	25.54%	12.77%	7.92%	0.19%
$25,000 up to $37,178	22.54%	11.27%	4.17%	-3.56%
$37,179 up to $74,356	31.68%	15.84%	15.59%	9.16%
$74,357 up to $77,961	37.44%	18.72%	22.79%	17.16%
$77,962 up to $120,887	38.01%	19.01%	23.14%	17.51%
$120,888 and over	42.40%	21.20%	28.62%	23.59%

Rates are federal, provincial, and territorial marginal tax rates combined. The rates include all surtaxes.

Assumption made that credits claimed are the basic personal amount and the low income tax reduction if applicable.

Eligible dividends are 1) those paid by Canadian public corporations and other corporations that are not CCPCs and are subject to general federal corporate tax rates and 2) income from CCPCs that is not investment income and is subject to general federal corporate tax rates.

Appendix 2

Complete Solutions for IPPs and RCAs

Marc Des Rosiers, FSA, FCIA is an actuary from Aperion Consulting in Toronto. Marc's twenty-six years of actuarial experience has helped many Canadians structure Individual Pension Plans (IPPs) and Retirement Compensation Arrangements (RCAs). His firm works with executives and business owners and provides them with complete solutions including advice, legal documents, filings, administration, and actuarial certification. Marc can be reached at (416) 628-3743 or mdr@retireware.com.

Index

13339593R00099

Made in the USA
Charleston, SC
02 July 2012